SOCIETY IN THE MIND

SOCIETY TODAY AND TOMORROW

General Editor: A. H. Halsey

*Fellow of Nuffield College and Head of the Department
of Social and Administrative Studies, Oxford*

*

THE SECONDARY MODERN SCHOOL

by William Taylor, *Principal Lecturer in Education, Bede College, Durham*

THE CUTTESLOWE WALLS: A Study in Social Class

by Peter Collison, *Department of Social and Administrative Studies, Oxford*

CRIME AND THE SOCIAL STRUCTURE

by John Barron Mays, *Senior Lecturer, Department of Social Science, University of Liverpool*

SOCIETY IN THE MIND: Elements of Social Eidos

by Charles Madge, *Professor of Sociology, University of Birmingham*

THE FAWLEY PRODUCTIVITY AGREEMENT

by Allan Flanders, *Senior Lecturer in Industrial Relations, University of Oxford*

SOCIETY IN THE MIND:
Elements of Social Eidos

by
CHARLES MADGE

FABER AND FABER LTD
24 Russell Square
London

First published in mcmlxiv
by Faber and Faber Limited
24 Russell Square, London, W.C.1
Printed in Great Britain by
Western Printing Services Limited, Bristol

© *Charles Madge*
1964

ACKNOWLEDGEMENTS

Acknowledgements are due to International Publishers, New York, for quotations from Roy Pascal's translation of *The German Ideology* by K. Marx and F. Engels; to the Hogarth Press and to W. W. Norton and Company, for quotations from J. Strachey's translation of *Civilization and Its Discontents* by S. Freud; to Jonathan Cape for quotations from A. Livingston's translation of *The Mind and Society* (*Trattato di Sociologia generale*) by V. Pareto; to the Free Press for quotations from *The Social System* by T. Parsons; and to the Clarendon Press, Oxford, for quotations from *Nuer Religion* by E. Evans-Pritchard.

I should also like to express thanks to those other authors who are quoted in my text and to their publishers.

C. M.

The logico-experimental sciences are made up of a sum of theories that are like living creatures, in that they are born, live, and die, the young replacing the old, the group alone enduring. As is the case with living beings, the lifetimes of theories vary in length and not always are the long-lived ones the ones that contribute most to the advancement of knowledge. Faith and metaphysics aspire to an ultimate, eternal resting-place. Science knows that it can attain only provisory, transitory positions. Every theory fulfils its function, and nothing more can be asked of it.

PARETO, *The Mind and Society*
vol. iv, p. 1729 (§ 2400)

On such subjects and with such starting points we must be content if we can draw a rough outline of the truth . . . for it is the mark of an educated mind to expect as much exactness in each kind of subject matter as its nature admits.

ARISTOTLE, *Nicomachean Ethics*, I. iii. 4

CONTENTS

CONTENTS

INTRODUCTION

Each of us has in his mind some sort of a picture (seldom clearly in focus) of society, just as he has a picture of the universe and a picture of himself.[1] If and when we scrutinize the picture, there become detached from it certain elements which I shall call ideas: an inexact word which will be readily understood. While it is possible to consider such ideas either cognitively or evaluatively, these aspects are seldom separated by anyone but a philosopher or a sociologist. I would describe their function as the validation, or invalidation, of social institutions. Validation can be considered cognitively as a form of explanation or evaluatively as a form of justification. The emphasis is now on one, now on the other, and in most everyday thinking and expression, the distinction simply does not arise.

In this book I am not concerned so much with specific social ideas as with something more general which I call *social eidos*. In my usage,[2] eidos, as a whole, means the predominant character of the whole stock of ideas available in a society or group. Social eidos then means that part of eidos which relates to social institutions and activities. Social membership has a pervasive effect on all thinking and social eidos

[1] 'A society is possible in the last analysis because the individuals in it carry around in their heads some sort of picture of that society.' Louis Wirth, Preface to Karl Mannheim, *Ideology and Utopia*, p. xxv.
[2] Adapted from that of Gregory Bateson, *Naven*. (Cambridge, 1936.)

therefore tends to spread over into eidos as a whole. But some ideas are more explicitly social than others and, among these, some are more cardinal than others. The focus, as it were, of the abstraction of social eidos rests upon the cardinal social ideas of a society or group, even though its full reference extends to peripheral social ideas and even to ideas which are not obviously social.

To illustrate this, and to give a starting point for the chapters that follow, I will attempt a provisional characterization of the social eidos of a 'modern' society like our own. It has two distinctive features. In it, firstly, society and its institutions are conceived in a historical perspective. Secondly, its preferred and basic method of validating social institutions is in terms which can be considered 'rational', in accordance with the standards of technical rationality that obtain generally in the basic employments of life.

Therefore the plan of this book will be to examine, first, the element of historical perspective in our contemporary social eidos and to outline very briefly its main empirical and conceptual foundations. Comte formulated a 'Law of the Three Stages' according to which all ideas, including social ideas, had passed through and were bound to pass through a religious, a metaphysical and finally a scientific stage. Sociology, as Comte saw it, was to be the embodiment of a scientific social eidos. There is a related perspective in Marxism and other nineteenth century social philosophies and theories of history. One has only to make the most casual scrutiny of our contemporary 'picture of society' to find that, in one form or another, this idea of stages is implied in it. We define the state of our society by comparing it with other societies which, as we see it, represent other stages of development. We define our own social eidos by contrasting it with what we know, or think we know, about the social eidos of these societies.

Part I of this book is intended to clarify the ideology of historical perspective and its place in our own social eidos—

not, I must emphasize, to provide a history of social eidos. Rather, I draw attention to what I feel to be the crucial turning points in its development. The three chapters correspond, however, with three hypothetical stages of social eidos, akin to those of Comte though not precisely his. Chapter I indicates how modern research and analysis has brought into greater familiarity the nature of primitive or archaic social eidos. Chapter II is concerned with the beginnings of speculative and moralizing thought in India, China and Greece. Chapter III summarizes, in some of its aspects, the effect on social eidos of the rise of the natural sciences in the seventeenth century.

In Part II, I turn to the other distinctive element in modern social eidos, the idea of the rational validation of social institutions. I comment on some pioneering attempts by sociologists and psychologists to analyse the part played by rational and non-rational elements in social thought and motivation.

In Part III, I develop the argument that, as well as other kinds of social structure, there can be mapped, in each society, a 'social structure of social eidos', owing to differences among the members in their access to social ideas and in the type of interest they take in them. I am also led to take a somewhat polemical stand against 'moralistic' tendencies in contemporary sociology. My personal utopia, it will be seen, is aesthetic rather than moral. But for the present we have to accept, unreservedly, the overriding claim of practical rationality, the rationality of survival.

This short book has cost me a good deal to write but it does not by any means set out to be definitive or comprehensive. Ranging as it does over many fields of knowledge and speculation, its inadequacies will be obvious to almost every kind of specialist. The student new to sociology will need to supplement it by reading widely in the sociological classics to which from time to time it refers. In dealing with special fields, such as those of the archaeologist and the historian of science, I have preferred to cite works which, though written for non-specialists, are none the less based on solid scholarship, such as Gordon Childe's *What Happened in History*, A. L. Basham's *The Wonder that was India* and H. Butterfield's *The Origins of Modern Science*.

A. Livingston's translation of Pareto's *The Mind and Society* has long been out of print, so I have quoted from it rather freely. The space devoted to Talcott Parsons may seem out of proportion to the rest of the book, but it is of course far less than would be needed for even a cursory treatment of the whole of his theory. I have concentrated mainly on the distinction he draws, which to me seems arbitrary, between social ideas and social values.

In writing this book, I have come across certain works which, even when I disagreed with them, impressed me deeply by their liberating quality, by the new avenues of thought and action which they seemed to open up. The early writings of Marx and the late writings of Freud have indeed this quality to an exceptional degree. So have the famous *Protestant Ethic* of Max Weber and Pareto's treatise on sociology. In their different ways, the second volume of Needham's *Science and Civilization in China* and Bachelard's *La Formation de l'Esprit Scientifique* have had a similar impact, and, in the realm of enlightened aesthetic utopias, so have Brown's *Life against Death* and Marcuse's *Eros and Civilization*. It is from starting points like these that I am hopeful we can begin to break out from the triviality and complacency of the 'third stage' of social eidos, but I have to emphasize that they are only starting points. To start to unblock our minds is something, but we still await clarifications that can only come from fundamental researches in human biology and psychology. Almost everything still remains to be discovered about the possible development of the human being and of human society.

Birmingham, October 1962.

PART I

Historical Perspective in Social Eidos

B

Chapter 1

ARCHAIC THOUGHT

We define our own style of thought, our eidos, by comparing or contrasting it with the eidos of other peoples
and other periods. As we learn more about the other kinds of
eidos, we appreciate better what it is that is distinctive in our
own. Our approach to the study of primitive people and their
eidos has become more scientific, more scholarly, more objective, more relativist, as time has gone on. In considering how
much we know about eidos and social eidos in primitive and
pre-industrial societies, it is wise to remember how painfully
this knowledge is being won, how closely our knowledge and
our ignorance are still bound up with the shifting limits and
resistances of our own thought.

I am calling *archaic* the ideas and bodies of ideas characteristic of primitive societies and also of early Bronze Age civilizations. Each primitive or archaic society has its own eidos, or
framework and style of thinking, but from a modern perspective the similarities between them are more striking than the
differences. The mental processes of primitives have long been
compared with those of children and psychotics but, suggestive
as such comparisons have proved, archaic thought, unlike the
thought of children or psychotics, is thought which has, in its
own way, been socialized and standardized. That is to say, it
depends on a body of ideas shared and accepted by the members
of a society and tested over generations against the realities of
the environment and of social intercourse. Archaic ideas,

19

however mistaken they may seem to us, were not so mistaken as to lead to the rapid extinction of those who held them. We must assume them to be viable in their own social context and complete in their own right.

When we look back over the recent history of scholarly attitudes to archaic thought, we can see a movement from ridicule to a sense of paradox and then to a growing understanding. What Sir James Frazer was inclined to describe as 'the quaint fancies of the lowest savages'[1] were, for Lévy-Bruhl, a subject for serious study and analysis. But he too betrayed the ethnocentric bias of his time in the title of his book, published in 1910, *Les Fonctions Mentales dans les Sociétés Inférieures*. His thesis was that primitive thought, though perplexing to us, had its own principles which were fundamentally different from those of modern thought. Over the next thirty years there was a general tendency, exemplified in Radin and Malinowski, to play down this difference. Primitive thought, though sometimes magical and mystical, was also, they were able to show, often practical and realistic. Freud and Pareto, among others, were at the other end of the scale, pointing out the continued importance of non-logical elements in the thought of modern societies. The art and sensibility of this period were also strongly tinged with primitivism. In a relatively short time, the gulf between civilized and primitive thought and feeling seemed to become bridgeable.

Lévy-Bruhl believed, as did Durkheim, that the study of archaic thought could throw light on the categories and logical principles of our modern thought. It is to their influence perhaps more than to any other that we owe the now pervasive idea that the categories of thought are *social* in origin. This is much the same as saying that *all* eidos is social eidos, and this in turn means that attention has been drawn to those aspects of thought and symbolization which reflect, or appear to reflect, social realities and forms. Thus, to Durkheim, the category of,

[1] Quoted by F. M. Cornford, *Principium Sapientiae*, p. 226.

ARCHAIC THOUGHT

the sacred and the idea of god reflect the supra-individual power of society. Looking at it the other way round, if one is to understand the specifically social eidos of an archaic society, then one is led to include in it the kind of magico-mystical thinking that Lévy-Bruhl seeks to explain by his 'Law of Participation' and that Durkheim, and following him Radcliffe-Brown and others, trace out in their analyses of totemism and its relation to the social structure.

Lévy-Bruhl begins his book on primitive thought by a paragraph on 'collective representations', a technical term introduced some years earlier by Durkheim to describe the 'pictures' (as I called them) which a group shares of those objects which have importance to it. These collective representations, he says 'are common to the members of a given social group; they are transmitted from one generation to another; they impress themselves upon its individual members, and awaken in them sentiments of respect, fear, adoration, and so on, according to the circumstances of the case'.[1] The collective representations of primitives, he goes on to say, 'differ very profoundly from our ideas or concepts', because of the mystico-magical view of reality which they imply. 'Not a single being or object or natural phenomenon in their collective representations is what it appears to be to our minds. For instance, to the primitive who belongs to a totemic community every animal, every plant, indeed every object, such as the sun, moon and stars, forms part of a totem, and has its own class and sub-class. Consequently, each individual has his special affinities, and possesses powers over the members of his totem, class and sub-class; he has obligations towards them, mystic relations with other totems, and so forth.'[2] He does not deny that primitive vocabularies include generic terms such as man, woman, dog, tree and so on, but he considers that, in contrast to our own concepts 'instead of being surrounded by an atmosphere of logical

[1] L. Lévy-Bruhl, (tr. L. Clare) *How Natives Think*, p. 13.
[2] *Ibid.*, p. 38.

21

potentiality, these representations welter, as it were, in an atmosphere of mystical possibilities'.[1]

Malinowski[2] and Radin,[3] both of whom, unlike Lévy-Bruhl, had first-hand experience of primitive societies, insisted that this was too sweeping. They had themselves observed and documented the magic and myth of primitive peoples, but they found, side by side with them, a fund of experimental knowledge and a practical orientation to the environment. Moreover the primitive could clearly distinguish between what was magic and what was not. In the Trobriand Islands, 'magic, performed officially by the garden magician under ceremonial conditions, by means of rite and spell and with the observance of taboos, forms a special department. Practical husbandry, on the other hand, carried out by each one with the aid of his hands and common sense, and based on the recognition of the causal relation between effort and achievement, constitutes another department. Magic is based on myth, practical work on empirical theory. The former aims at forestalling unaccountable mishaps and procuring undeserved good luck, the latter supplies what human effort is known naturally to bring about. The first one is a sociological prerogative of the leader, the *towosi*; the second is the economic duty of every member of the community.'[4] There are, according to Radin, 'two general types of temperament among primitive peoples, that of the priest-thinker and that of the layman; the one only secondarily identified with action, the other primarily so; the one interested in the analysis of the religious phenomena, the other in their effect'.[5] Lévy-Bruhl himself found the mystical and prelogical element in the collective representations of primitives 'particularly in those relating to their institutions and religious beliefs';[6]

---

[1] *Ibid.*, p. 126.

[2] See, for example, his essay, 'Magic, Science and Religion' in *ed.* J. Needham, *Science, Religion and Reality*, 1925.

[3] For example, in *Primitive Man as Philosopher*, 1927, p. 28.

[4] B. Malinowski, *Coral Gardens and their Magic*, vol. I, p. 77.

[5] P. Radin, *Primitive Religion*, p. 14.   [6] L. Lévy-Bruhl, *op. cit.*, p. 122.

it is more marked, therefore, in their social eidos than in their general eidos. The layman does not often think about his social institutions but when he does so he tends to think of them in mystical terms, along lines laid down by mystical specialists. In his last book, *L'Expérience Mystique et les Symboles chez les Primitifs* (1938), Lévy-Bruhl notes the existence of such specialists in every primitive society, however simple.[1] A full analysis of the relation between magical, religious and social eidos would have to take account of the wide variation to be found in the status of those considered to be specialists in these fields. Magicians, priests, prophets, chiefs, elders have rôles that vary from one society to another, that are sometimes distinct and sometimes overlap.

The initiation of the young males at puberty, (and also, with less emphasis, of the young females) seems to be a universal feature of primitive societies. 'The simplest tribes, the food-gatherers and fish-hunting peoples' to quote Radin[2] 'have already developed intricate and complex rites around it. They are fundamental and basic rites of mankind.' Lévy-Bruhl in his first book was already pointing out that 'in most of the primitive peoples we know, there are personages who undergo an additional initiation. These are the wizards, medicine-men, shamans, doctors, or whatever else they may be called'.[3] For them the rites are similar but more extreme, and their mystical knowledge and powers are correspondingly increased. Many initiation rites are painful and terrifying; those who take part in them are in an excited and suggestible state; the whole atmosphere, deliberately cultivated, is one of magical illusion. This is partly what Lévy-Bruhl had in mind in his initial description of collective representations, quoted above. These, which might be considered as cardinal elements in primitive eidos, are esoteric; in many cases, women and children are not supposed to know anything about them. Initiated adults are made to feel that they have been given some understanding of them, but that a fuller understanding is reserved for the older men and,

[1] p. 31.   [2] P. Radin, *op. cit.*, p. 79.   [3] L. Lévy-Bruhl, *op. cit.*, p. 354.

above all, for specialists who have had a fuller initiation. The specialists, whose special knowledge gives them power and makes them feared, are also the custodians, formulators and elaborators of eidos in its esoteric aspect and they have a vested interest in its mysteriousness.

Gregory Bateson has described[1] for the Iatmul people of New Guinea what he calls their *eidos* or characteristic pattern of intellectual activity; it is from his book that I have taken this term. The Iatmul are a primitive people with complicated religious and social institutions. They have shamans and sorcerers, but it is part of the general male ethos to prize erudition, for example about names and totems. A learned man carries in his head between ten and twenty thousand names. More specifically, to quote Bateson, 'Iatmul thought is characterized not only by its intellectuality, but also by a tendency to insist that what is symbolically, sociologically, or emotionally true, is also cognitively true. Apparently the sort of paradox which can be constructed in this way is very attractive to the Iatmul mind, and the same mental twist is, of course, recognisable in dialecticians and theologians in all parts of the world. Among the Iatmul the dialecticians and theologians are not a class apart but are . . . the chief contributors to the culture. Thus it comes about that many of the complications of the culture can be described as *tours-de-force* played upon this type of paradox, devices which stress the contradiction between emotional and cognitive reality or between different aspects of emotional truth'. For example: 'Only the more erudite men know that *mwai* (long-nosed masks) and *mbwatnggowi* (ceremonial dolls) are really *wagan* (spiritual beings); and when they told me of this they spoke of it as of a mystery which was beyond their comprehension, a paradox which had to be accepted and at which they marvelled with a certain serious humility and acceptance of its incomprehensibility.'[2]

[1] G. Bateson, *Naven*. 1936. 'Naven' is a ceremony of central importance for the Iatmul.   [2] *Ibid.*, p. 233.

Such assertions of identity between quite different kinds of things are much stressed by Lévy-Bruhl as a distinguishing feature of primitive mentality and one which can only be explained by regarding this mentality as 'prelogical'. Thus he quotes Lumholtz's account of the Huichol Indians, who believe that corn, deer and hikuli (a sacred plant) are one and the same thing. Among the same people 'a great variety of objects are considered as plumes. Clouds, cotton wool, the white tail of a deer, the deer's antlers, and even the deer itself are considered as plumes, and all serpents are believed to have plumes. . . . Everyone who kills a deer comes into possession of a precious plume, that insures him health and luck. Not only the antler, but the whole body of the deer is, in the Huichol mind, a plume, just as a bird is called a plume. . . . Lumholtz is very emphatic on this point: to the Huichols the deer *is* hikuli, the hikuli *is* corn, the corn *is* a plume. . . . From the standpoint of logical thought, such "identities" are, and remain unintelligible. One entity is the symbol of another, but not that other.'[1]

Evans-Pritchard has recently discussed this problem in relation to similar statements of identity among the Nuer. He writes: 'It seems odd, if not absurd, to a European when he is told that a twin is a bird as though it were an obvious fact, for Nuer are not saying that a twin is like a bird but that he is a bird. . . . But, in fact, no contradiction is involved in the statement, which, on the contrary appears quite sensible, and even true, to one who presents the idea to himself in the Nuer language and within their system of religious thought. . . . They are not saying that a twin has a beak, feathers and so forth. Nor in their everyday relations with twins do Nuer speak of them as birds or act towards them as though they were birds. They treat them as what they are, men and women. But in addition to being men and women they are of a twin-birth, and a twin-birth is a special revelation of Spirit: and Nuer express

[1] Lévy-Bruhl, *op. cit.*, p. 122 *et seq*. The examples are from C. Lumholtz, *Symbolism of the Huichol Indians* and *Unknown Mexico*.

25

this special character of twins in the "twins are birds" formula because twins and birds, though for different reasons, are both associated with Spirit and this makes twins, like birds, "people of the above" and "children of God", and hence a bird a suitable symbol in which to express the special relationship in which a twin stands to God.'[1]

This more than purely analogical symbolism, in which an element A is persistently stated to be not analogous with but identical with another element B, is clearly an important feature of archaic magical and religious thought. Its very mysteriousness gives it an esoteric force. It is an integral part of primitive social eidos as expressed, for example, in the institutions of totemism. At a simple magical level, it involves, shall we say, pretending that one thing is another, willing it to be another. At a religious level, it involves the unifying idea of Spirit, as in Evans-Pritchard's example above, or in Bateson's where dolls and masks were both, in some mysterious way, 'spiritual beings'. At the level of social eidos, and for the validation of social institutions, it may, as in the totem, provide a kind of embodied metaphor of the distinctness of different social groups. Members of one clan, for example, have by and large the same physical appearance as members of another clan, but spiritually they are different. From this difference proceed different obligations, social and ritual, of action and avoidance. The difference is emphasized and symbolized by the parallel but in this case visible differences of totemic species. Towards these, too, there are obligations of action and avoidance. There is a totemic ancestor as well as a human ancestor. These are at a higher level of generality, and of spirituality, than ordinary individuals: the totemic ancestor may in fact be conceived as the spirit of the species, the human ancestor as the spirit of the clan.

Durkheim regarded totemism as in itself a religion, 'the most primitive one that is now observable' and 'inseparable from a

[1] E. Evans-Pritchard, *Nuer Religion* (1956), p. 131.

social organization on a clan basis'.[1] For Durkheim,—'before all ... (religion) is a system of ideas with which the individuals represent to themselves the society of which they are members, and the obscure but intimate relations which they have with it'.[2] Evans-Pritchard comments: 'Sociological theories of religion ... have sought to understand primitive religions ... as products of social life. (They) have shown successfully that many features of these religions can be understood only by sociological analysis, by relating them to the social structure. This is true of Nuer religion. ... But Durkheim and his colleagues and pupils were not content to say that religion, being part of the social life, is strongly influenced by the social structure. They claimed that the religious conceptions of primitive peoples are nothing more than a symbolic representation of the social order. It is (they say) his society that primitive man worships in the symbol of a god. It is to his society that he prays and makes a sacrifice. This postulate of sociologistic metaphysic seems to me to be an assertion for which evidence is totally lacking. It was Durkheim and not the savage who made society into a god.'[3]

Evans-Pritchard's criticism is justified. Religious ideas are elaborated in a social context and used for social purposes but this does not mean that they can be wholly explained in sociological terms. Moreover, once invented, religious conceptions exert an influence of their own, independent from that of society, indeed often driving men away from society, or forcing them into conflict with it. None the less, it is indisputable that religious ideas, rituals and institutions are intertwined with primitive social eidos, and, if we make allowance for his terminology, there is little doubt of the correctness of Comte's thesis

[1] E. Durkheim, *The Elementary Forms of the Religious Life*, p. 167.
[2] *Ibid.*, p. 225.
[3] E. Evans-Pritchard, *op. cit.*, p. 313. The suffix '-istic' in 'sociologistic' implies undue emphasis on a particular intellectual approach, in this case that of sociology. For Evans-Pritchard's usage of 'metaphysic' compare the footnote on p. 65 below.

that human knowledge passed through a 'theological' stage, introduced by an initial period of 'pure Fetichism, which allowed free exercise to that tendency of our nature by which Man conceives of all external bodies as animated by a life analogous to his own, with differences of mere intensity'.[1] Lévy-Bruhl and Durkheim had at their disposal (to quote the former) 'an immense mass of documents dealing with the institutions, customs, and languages of so-called savage or primitive races'[2] which had accumulated since Comte's day and which they were able to use for what, in essence, was a confirmation of his thesis and a completion of his programme. Durkheim also follows Comte in thinking that all religions, including the most primitive, have been appropriate to their own social conditions and, by implication, that religious sentiment towards the social bond can and should find expression also in our own secular epoch. Comte projected his 'Religion of Humanity' in the same spirit as Durkheim when, in Evans-Pritchard's phrase, he 'made society into a god.'

Comte's own account of the 'fetichistic' sub-stage hardly goes beyond the kind of conjectural pre-history that was current throughout the Enlightenment. For example his reference to the 'metaphorical constitution of human language' being 'a remarkable and eternal testimony to the primitive condition of Man'[3] can be paralleled in Condorcet's statement that 'In the infancy of language nearly every word is a metaphor and every phrase an allegory. The mind grasps the figurative and the literal sense simultaneously'.[4] Fetichism, Comte says, 'favoured the poetic and artistic development of humanity, by transferring the human sense of existence to all external objects. . . . The external world can never since have been in such familiar accordance with the soul of Man as when all that he saw was

---

[1] A. Comte, *The Positive Philosophy*, tr. H. Martineau, vol. II, p. 186.
[2] L. Lévy-Bruhl, *op. cit.*, p. 16.   [3] A. Comte, *op. cit.* vol. II, p. 190.
[4] A-N de Condorcet, *The Progress of the Human Mind*, tr. J. Barraclough, p. 37.

alive with his life, and subordinated to his destiny' and in evidence of this he refers to 'the too rare fragments of fetich poetry
which have come down to us, or over from distant tribes'.[1]
This notion, and the general drift of his account of the fetichistic stage, Comte may owe in part, directly or indirectly, to
Vico. More than a hundred years earlier, the Neapolitan
philosopher had written: 'The most sublime labor of poetry
is to give sense and passion to insensate things; and it is characteristic of children to take inanimate things in their hands and
talk to them in play as if they were living persons. This philo-
logico-philosophical axiom proves to us that in the world's
childhood men were by nature sublime poets.'[2] Moreover Vico
adduces anthropological evidence in support of his view.
'This' he writes, 'is now confirmed by the American Indians,
who call gods all the things that surpass their small understanding. We may add the ancient Germans dwelling about
the Arctic Ocean, of whom Tacitus tells that they spoke of
hearing the sun pass at night from west to east through the
sea, and affirmed that they saw the gods. These very rude and
simple nations help us to a much better understanding of the
founders of the gentile world . . . '.[3]

The fetichistic sub-stage of human development is seen by
Comte as one in which all the main branches of human activity
—religion, the fine arts, political organization, industry—
already existed in embryo, but in an undifferentiated state. It
was least favourable, he thought, to natural philosophy—
'Fetichism obstructs all advance in genuine knowledge. . . .
At this period of intellectual infancy, imaginary facts wholly
overwhelm real ones. . . . The mind is in a state of vague pre-
occupation with regard to the external world, which, universal
and natural as it is, is not the less a kind of permanent halluci-
nation, proceeding from such a preponderance of the affective

[1] A. Comte, op. cit. vol. II, p. 215.
[2] G. Vico, The New Science, tr. T. G. Bergin and M. H. Fisch, p. 64.
[3] Ibid., p. 104.

over the intellectual life, that the most absurd beliefs impair all direct observation of natural phenomena.'[1] Religion, he thinks, though all pervading at this stage, was not institutionally differentiated; it was 'of a kind that required every man to be his own priest'.[2] Political and moral institutions, though they existed, were also relatively undeveloped. It was to the fine arts and to poetry that fetichism was most propitious. In effect, Comte is saying that in its origins religion is suffused with poetic fantasy. One may compare Durkheim: 'the truth is that there is a poetry inherent in all religion'.[3] In his discussion of the problem of symbols in primitive religion, Evans-Pritchard says that one reason why they have been misunderstood 'is that the poetic sense of primitive peoples has not been sufficiently allowed for'.[4]

In reviewing the whole movement of learned and literary ideas about the primitive since the Enlightenment, two tendencies can be discerned. The first is the tendency towards objectivity and away from ethnocentric bias: this is in keeping with the scientific, rational, critical trend of the period. But the other tendency, already explicit in Vico, is to seek in the archaic and primitive an element of poetry which is felt to be disappearing from the modern world. This tendency is obvious enough among modern artists and poets, but it has, I think, also motivated anthropologists, historians and scholars and has entered into their interpretations, and into the interest of a wide public in their work. Along with the shift to rationality, and partly because of it, there has been a broad nostalgic turning back towards what is, psychologically, the lost world of childhood: what Vico called 'the world's childhood.' It is of course possible for the two tendencies to be united: it is possible to be both nostalgic *and* objective. And though the problem of how to restore what is felt to have been lost is presumably insoluble, the utopian hope of restoring it is a spur to social invention.

---

[1] A. Comte, *op. cit.* vol. II, p. 194.   [2] *Ibid.*, vol. II, p. 192.
[3] E. Durkheim, *op. cit.*, p. 382.   [4] E. Evans-Pritchard, *op. cit.*, p. 142.

The assumption has been, from Vico onwards, that we could reconstruct the eidos of remote pre-history from that of surviving primitive tribes. Forming a link between them and classical antiquity, the civilizations of ancient Egypt and Mesopotamia have seemed to embody, on a grand scale, the archaism of primitive eidos. Our knowledge of these civilizations has only recently been transformed by modern archaeology, and broad interpretations of the archaeological evidence tend to base themselves on one or another of the main varieties of social theory. Thus if one turns to the account given by Gordon Childe in *What Happened in History*, one is soon aware that Marxist categories and causal explanations are being applied to the Bronze Age evidence, and applied to very good effect. Or if one reads the essay on 'Myth and Reality', by H. and H. A. Frankfort, in *Before Philosophy*, one is conscious of the influence of Durkheim and Lévy-Bruhl on their survey of the logic of myth in ancient Egypt and Babylon. When scholars raise their eyes from detail and take a broad view, they are more likely to take over one of the ordering ideas of their time than to invent a new one. The non-specialist thus gets his information about the remote past subtly influenced, as often as not, by the very recent past. This limitation must be borne in mind in reading the paragraphs that follow.

We can conveniently use as chronological framework the simple scheme set out by Gordon Childe[1] beginning with 'the first two thousand years of civilization' which 'coincide with what archaeologists describe as the Bronze Age'. This was the age of the first cities, the first concentration of population, and the invention of writing. 'Copper and bronze were the only metals used for tools and weapons' but these were 'so expensive as normally to be available only to gods, kings, chiefs and the employees of Temples and States'.[2] From about 3000 B.C., 'imposing State organizations' were built up in the Nile, Tigris-Euphrates and Indus valleys. Soon after 2300 B.C. these

[1] In the first chapter of *What Happened in History*.   [2] *Op. cit.*, p. 24.

disintegrated, to re-emerge in Egypt and Mesopotamia but not in India. 'The rejuvenated civilizations of . . . the Second Millennium differ from their parents of the Third most significantly in the greater prominence of a middle class of merchants, professional soldiers, clerks, priests and skilled artizans, no longer embedded in "great households" but subsisting independently.'[1] New centres of civilization arose in China, Asia Minor (the Hittites), Syria (the Phoenicians), Crete and Mycenaean Greece. About 1200 B.C. the Bronze Age came to an end amid general cataclysm, and the introduction of iron tools and weapons.

Childe notes the poverty of cultural achievements 'during the fifteen odd centuries of the full Bronze Age . . . compared with the brilliant achievements of the Fourth Millennium and the organization of civilization itself.' This lengthy epoch of large-scale city-centred State organization he characterizes as essentially conservative. The 'social thought' of this time is inextricably interwoven with its religious thought. Both in its themes and its logic, the socio-religious ideology of Bronze Age Egypt and Mesopotamia has obvious affinities with what we have described as archaic thought: identification of man, god and animal: ritual respect and avoidance.

At length the diffusion of an economic technique for 'producing in bulk iron of good quality' brought in a new epoch. 'Cheap iron democratized agriculture and industry and warfare too. Any peasant could afford an iron axe to clear fresh land for himself and iron ploughshares wherewith to break up strong ground. The common artizan could own a kit of metal tools that made him independent of the households of kings, gods or nobles. With iron weapons a commoner could meet on more equal terms the Bronze Age knight. With them too poor and backward barbarians could challenge the armies of civilized States whose monopoly of bronze armaments had made them seem invulnerable'.[2]

The invasion of civilized states by uncivilized peoples led to

[1] *Ibid.*, p. 155.   [2] *Ibid.*, p. 183.

a period of dislocation but not complete discontinuity. The re-emerging civilizations of the Iron Age retain the distinctive heritage of the Bronze Age. They are ruled by absolute kings whose status is either semi-divine or at least bound up in the dominant religious system. Some first elements of 'democratization' were apparent in the Bronze Age, and these became more extensive in the Iron Age. The new civilizations were more secular and less magical. As though in response to their increasing social complexity, there arose in their midst a new type of thinker and a new type of thought, making it plausible to see this point of history as marking a new 'stage' in the development of social eidos.

Chapter 2

THE TEACHERS OF MORALITY

In different parts of the civilized world there are still found in full force, or were found until very recently, such archaisms as the worship of spirits, the worship of ancestors, a ritual respect for certain animals, such as the cow, and a ritual avoidance of certain animals, such as the pig. These are all obvious enough in China, Japan, India and the Near East. Attenuated and rationalized they have their analogues in Christian beliefs and rituals. The continuities and correspondences are well known and need not lead to argument between believer and unbeliever. What we must attempt to characterize, however, is the development in thought which separates the social eidos of modern society from the archaic eidos we have been discussing.

During the First Millennium, as has often been pointed out, the idea of the great teacher comes increasingly to the fore. From this period date Zoroastrianism (? 1000 B.C.), the Hebrew prophets (eighth century), the Upanishads (seventh century), Buddhism and Jainism (sixth century), Confucianism and Taoism (sixth to third centuries) and the Ionian philosophers (sixth century). These developments were largely independent of each other and took place under widely differing circumstances. The teachings, too, were different, but what was similar was the emergence of institutions through whose means the teacher and his disciples could develop and transmit a body of teaching, and acquire a high moral prestige.

With or without supernatural legitimation, these teachings

owed much of their force to the idea of the great man, the saviour, the inspired teacher in whom they originated. As Freud expressed it: 'The super-ego of any given epoch of civilization originates in the same way as that of an individual; it is based on the impression left behind them by great leading personalities, men of outstanding force of mind, or men in whom some one human tendency has developed in unusual strength and purity, often for that reason very disproportionately.'[1]

To begin with, the teachers necessarily made use of concepts and idioms both of thought and ritual which they had inherited from the archaic epoch. This heritage, with much accretion and constant reinterpretation, remains embedded in the systems of thought which have come down from them to the present day. In interaction with the varying types of society in which they arose, the systems of thought developed on such distinctive lines that (in spite of some cross-fertilization) each appears as though a separate answer to a common need, namely the need of a rationale for man's existence in the context of Iron Age society, with its new flexibility and individualism.

At this stage of development, the analysis of social thought has obviously become more complex than that of earlier thought. It is no longer possible, even as an approximation, to postulate a particular system of thought as being the thought of a particular society. Even in a primitive society, some people are so to speak specialized in the field of social and related spiritual formulations. This specialization becomes elaborated in the Bronze Age civilizations. But as they mature, and even more in the Iron Age, though specialization continues there is also democratization especially for the middle ranks of society. In the early stages of civilization, esoteric knowledge is confined to the upper ranks, available to the multitude in visual and ritual forms and in myth. At the stage we are now considering, however, the formulations put forward by the new kind of teacher are designed for a society in which the middle ranks are

[1] S. Freud, *Civilization and its Discontents*, p. 137.

35

becoming more numerous, less dependent, better educated. Teachers will gain most following and have most prospect of continuing influence if they can appeal at all levels, upper, middle and popular. One criterion for success in a new socio-religious system is therefore that it should resolve, or appear to resolve, tensions in the structure of social stratification.

It would however be an impoverished view of this many-sided development if we saw in it only a force making for social and political integration. There is a strong tendency for some teachers and their followers to seek a solution on the plane of thought outside society, an individual rather than a social solution therefore. The development of the hermitage and the monastery belong to this epoch. It must be noted also that even for those who remain in the world the idea of a personal salvation becomes important. Such ideas, conceived in hermitages, become part of the idiom of personal religion within society. Where the tone of thought is more rational, less mystical, it may be more appropriate to speak of 'philosophy' than of 'religion' in this context. The individual teacher or thinker is institutionally separate from the State, though he may develop his own schools, corporations or religious orders and though he may seek and obtain patronage and protection from rulers.

Moreover it becomes possible for different teachers to provide simultaneously within a society different philosophies or doctrines. The history of thought is thus increasingly the history of interaction of different schools of thought, as well as the interdependence between thought and society. Each system, each school, bears the impress of individual, original thought. But in order to survive in an acceptable form, over time they tend to become socially and politically conformist. Changing political needs lead to changing interpretations of the original system of thought.

We can illustrate these generalizations briefly from three post-Bronze Age civilizations, those of ancient India, China and Greece.

By the later Vedic period (900–500 B.C.), the Aryan tribes were consolidated into small kingdoms, and there had been a great development of the royal horse sacrifice. The doctrine of the transmigration of souls appears for the first time, according to some scholars as the result of shamanistic influence from Central Asia. But 'to the greater minds of the time . . . rebirth in heaven was not enough—a way had to be found to escape the cycle of birth and death altogether. It was found . . . in knowledge, achieved by much meditation and asceticism . . . By the time of the Upanishads (800–700 B.C.) asceticism had become very widespread, and it was through the ascetics, rather than the orthodox sacrificial priests, that the new teachings developed and spread. Some ascetics were solitary psychopaths, dwelling in the depths of the forests, and suffering self-inflicted tortures of hunger, thirst, heat, cold and rain. Others dwelt in "penance grounds", on the outskirts of towns, where, like some of the less reputable holy men of later times, they would indulge in fantastic self-torture, sitting near blazing fires in the hot sun, lying on beds of thorns and spikes, hanging for hours head downwards from the branches of trees, or holding their arms motionless above their heads until they atrophied.

'Most of the new developments in thought, however, came from ascetics of less rigorous regimen, whose chief practices were the mental and spiritual exercises of meditation. Some of these dwelt alone on the outskirts of towns and villages, while others lived in groups of huts, under the leadership of an elder. Others wandered, often in large groups, begging alms, proclaiming their doctrines to all who wished to listen, and disputing with their rivals. Some were completely naked, while others wore simple garments.'[1]

The most influential religio-philosophical literature of ancient India derives from teachers of this kind. 'The term Upanishad means literally "a session," sitting at the feet of a master who imparts esoteric doctrines.'[2] While the earlier of these seek to

[1] A. L. Basham, *The Wonder that was India*, p. 243 *et seq.*   [2] *Ibid.*, p. 250.

37

explain the ritual of the horse sacrifice in cosmic and speculative terms, a later Upanishad is definitely critical of those who seek salvation by sacrifice.

'Abiding manifoldly in ignorance, they, all the same, like immature children think to themselves: "We have accomplished our aim." Since the performers of sacrificial ritual do not realise the truth because of passion, therefore, they, the wretched ones, sink down from heaven when the merit which qualified them for the higher world becomes exhausted. . . .

'Those who practice penance and faith in the forest, the tranquil ones, the knowers of truth, living the life of wandering mendicancy—they depart, freed from passion, through the door of the sun, to where dwells, verily, that immortal Purusha, the imperishable Soul.'[1]

These earliest philosophers—they precede those of Ionia and ancient China—were seeking by thought and meditation to understand the nature of existence and of the soul and of the relation between the two, and by this understanding to achieve release for the individual from sorrow and suffering in this and future lives. They were Brahmins, and their ideas were later embodied in the philosophies of orthodox Hinduism. But there were also a number of heterodox philosophies—materialist, atomist, fatalist, antinomian and sceptic—which ran counter to the main trend of Hinduism, and out of these controversies arose two important new religious systems, those of Jainism and Buddhism.

'It must be emphasized that the salvation promised by these teachers, and by others like them, was not dependent on the mere acceptance of the doctrine on the word of the teacher, or on belief in it on a cool logical basis. To achieve release from transmigration it was necessary that the fundamental doctrine should be realized in the inmost being of the individual, and such a realization could only be achieved by the mystical and ascetic practices generally known in the West as Yoga. Each

[1] (*Compiled by*) W. T. de Bary and others. *Sources of Indian Tradition*, p. 28.

group, even that of the materialists who followed Ajita, had its special system of meditation and mental or spiritual exercises, each its organized body of followers, usually ascetics, pledged to strive together for emancipation. Lay devotees and patrons were generally thought to be on the lowest rungs of the spiritual ladder, and there was little or no chance of full salvation outside the disciplined order.'[1]

This other worldly emphasis has remained a dominant feature of Indian culture down to the present day. For its strength to be maintained, the effective organization of monastic orders was one solution, provided that these did not become too isolated from society and therefore unable to recruit new members or defend themselves against enemies.

After a period in which Buddhism was in the ascendant in India (roughly from 300 B.C. to A.D. 300), Brahminical Hinduism was able to reassert itself. Formulae were found which reconciled the other worldly emphasis with the requirements of society. Such were the division of man's life into four stages of which the second, the longest, was to be devoted to his duties as a married man and householder, leaving till old age the retreat from the world and the life of contemplation; and the doctrine of Karma-Yoga, the yoga of action, as put forward in the *Bhagavad Gita* of which the theme is that:

'Action as such, is not detrimental to one's attainment of his spiritual goal. It is only one's attachment to the fruits of action that keeps one eternally involved in the cycle of birth and death. The *Gita*, therefore, teaches the art of "acting and yet not acting," i.e. acting without becoming personally involved in the action.'[2]

The revived form of Hinduism has remained essentially the same down to the present day. From this point on the superiority of the Brahmin and the authority of the scriptures were unquestioned and the caste system became more elaborate and rigid.

[1] *Ibid.*, p. 44.   [2] *Ibid.*, p. 281.

The evolution of ancient Chinese thought seems to take place smoothly from what Arthur Waley[1] has called the 'auguristic-sacrificial' stage, essentially archaic, into the stage of moral philosophy. Wisdom is to be found by approximation to the rulers and sages of the semi-mythical past, with the help of such books as the Book of History, the Book of Odes, the Book of Changes and the Book of Rites. An idealized past is an element common to most Chinese philosophies. By contrast with those of India, these are not concerned with the relationship of God and the soul, and show no theological development. There is a corresponding emphasis on the relationship of society and the individual. Except under the influence of Mahayana Buddhism, Chinese thinkers are not concerned with salvation in another world. Characteristically they are concerned with the establishment of harmony in this world, harmony between the natural and the social order, harmony of the individual and the social order (Confucius), harmony of the individual and the natural order (Taoism), harmony of the individual and his own nature (Mencius).

'Between 550 and 280 B.C. the enduring fundamental influences in the Chinese social order and in the whole intellectual life of China had their original.'[2] In China, as in Greece and India, a whole range of philosophies appeared in the course of two or three centuries, and the norm of philosophic speculation and controversy was established. In China, it may be tentatively explained as arising from a wish to restore and preserve 'harmony' within society, at a time when the authority of the first post-Bronze Age dynasty, the Chou, was crumbling. The philosophers could either attempt reform by persuasion, like Confucius and Mencius; or they could withdraw from active social participation, like the Taoists. Confucius emphasizes social correctness, which depends on having correct feelings which in turn are helped by correct observance of rituals. The

[1] A. Waley, The Way and its Power, p. 21.
[2] W. Eberhard, A History of China, p. 40.

Taoists emphasize simplicity, non-intervention, and psychological exercises akin to yoga.[1] Confucianism therefore is more suitable as a philosophy of orthodoxy, but in taking shape it incorporates elements of Taoism. There were other philosophies as well, as diverse as those of the Realists, who rejected traditionalism and exalted the State and war; and the Mohists, who taught pacifism and universal love.

Philosophic discussion has gone on through the centuries, but in China, as in India, there was established in the early centuries of our era an orthodox tradition of values and of social organization. There was room for gradual shifts of emphasis within this orthodoxy but not for major change. Under the Han dynasty was begun the system of examinations for the administrative services, based on the study of Confucian and other classic texts. These, through changing dynasties, have provided an enduring element, together with the 'scholar gentry', the social stratum in whose education they formed the main component, and who provided recruits for the imperial administration.

In the case of ancient China and India, there is much that scholarship has still to unravel. Each constitutes a separate, strange, unfamiliar and complex tradition. When we turn to Graeco-Roman civilization, from which our own derives, we enter a field of study which has long held a privileged position in Western scholarship. We have a special involvement in it which both motivates our interest and may make it difficult for us to view it in perspective. In interpreting this material, we are interpreting ourselves.

At about the same time that late nineteenth-century scholars were becoming interested in the mentality of primitives, in the myths of Egypt and Mesopotamia, in the ancient civilization

---

[1] Dr. Needham has stressed the importance of Taoism in the origins of Chinese science and technology, and has shown that its concepts were largely of shamanistic origin. See J. Needham, *Science and Civilization in China*, vol. II, Chapter 10.

of India and China—in general, that is, in fields of thought and expression *outside* the European tradition—they began also to look at the classical Graeco-Roman heritage afresh, emphasizing not only its advances but its links with the primitive and the un-Western. Nietzsche had written of a Dionysian, ecstatic element in Greek culture side by side with the Apollonian, rational element. Jane Harrison, in her pioneering *Prolegomena to the Study of Greek Religion* (1903), drew attention to the 'substratum of religious conceptions' that was 'at once more primitive and more permanent' than the 'splendid surface' of Homer and the poets. This was an anthropological viewpoint relatively new to classical scholarship, and owing much to the researches of Sir James Frazer, author of *The Golden Bough* (1900).

Another Cambridge scholar, F. M. Cornford, was influenced by the ideas of Durkheim and his collaborators when in *From Religion to Philosophy* (1912) he offered a sociological analysis of 'the origins of western speculation' in the philosophies of ancient Greece. Cornford suggested that when the Homeric, Olympian theology became obsolete, the philosophers took as their new starting point the archaic conceptions that pre-dated it. There were two main philosophic traditions, the one more mystical, the other more scientific, but the two strands are not really separable and the whole effort of the Greek intellect is towards their reconciliation.

Thus Thales of Miletus (*fl.* 585 B.C.) was styled by Aristotle the founder of philosophy and of science. Yet in spite of his reputation for the pursuit of practical knowledge, he 'immediately announces that the ultimate "nature" of all things is water, and that the universe is alive—"has soul in it" (ἔμψυχον)—and is full of spirits or Gods'.[1] The 'nature (φύσις) discussed by the Milesian philosophers as their primary datum is an archaic concept in which characteristically there has been no separation between the spiritual and the material.

[1] F. M. Cornford, *From Religion to Philosophy*, p. 4.

42

As well as mystical scientists like Thales we find scientific mystics like Pythagoras. He taught the transmigration of souls and a form of religious asceticism. The teaching of his school was partly religious, partly scientific. Its development of mathematics, and of the mathematical basis of music, was motivated by an interest in the mystical properties of numbers. In this book, Cornford emphasized the link between the Greek mystical philosophers and the mystery religion of Orphism. The evidence about Orphism is, however, scanty and in his last, posthumously published book Cornford advanced the striking theory that shamanistic influences had reached Greece from the north and that Pythagoras was one of a line of Greek shamans.[1]

Cornford describes Plato as having made 'the last and greatest attempt to formulate the mystical faith in rational terms',[2] and he equates the Platonic 'Forms' or 'Ideas' with the 'species-deities' of archaic thought, as described by Tylor.[3] Yet Plato, for all his mystical tendencies, is of course at the same time an intellectualist and rationalist. His great pupil and philosophical opponent, Aristotle, was far less mystical in temperament. Yet he too conceived the universe, or φύσις, as an entity that was in some sense alive.[4] The philosophies of Plato and Aristotle, though moving towards logic and science, retained enough mystical archaism to provide a basis for the philosophy, theology and mysticism of medieval Christendom and Islam. It is perhaps because the mystical and the rational are so fused in Greek philosophy that it did not immediately herald the development of the natural sciences but, instead, became a source of intellectual strength to the universal religions. This would also help to explain why, when eventually the natural sciences developed, the motivation of the early scientists was so largely religious and magical.

[1] F. M. Cornford, *Principium Sententiae*, p. 88. See also E. R. Dodds, *The Greeks and the Irrational*, p. 135 *et seq.*

[2] *From Religion to Philosophy*, p. 242.

[3] E. Tylor, *Primitive Culture* (1903), II, p. 243.

[4] See the quotation from his *Metaphysics* in Cornford, *op. cit.*, p. 135.

THE TEACHERS OF MORALITY

The 'great teachers' who introduced the second stage of social eidos represented the idea of moral authority based on moral personality. They were more moral and less magical than the priests, shamans and sacred rulers of the archaic stage. In their teaching also there were rational and intellectual elements which were to be intensified in the third stage. The magical role still clung to them, the scientific role was in a few cases developed. In fact these teachers were often more magical in their scientific aspect, less magical in their rational-moral aspect. Morality and 'ultimate value' can perhaps be seen as the invention of the second stage and our special heritage from it.

Chapter 3

NATURAL SCIENCE AND THE LAW
OF THE THREE STAGES

The modern development of the natural sciences took place in the west, not in India or China. One is bound to connect this historical fact with the distinctive character of the Greek eidos. In the ancient western world, the Great Teacher who came closest to the outlook of modern natural science was Aristotle. But after his death, there ensued a long period—some nineteen centuries—during which philosophic speculation was at a low ebb and scientific knowledge remained almost stationary or retrogressed. The Greek philosophers did indeed leave a permanent succession carrying on their intellectual activity for the benefit of a small, learned minority. For the majority a broader teaching was supplied by the universalist religions of Christendom and Islam. The rise and sway of these religions—which combined Greek and Jewish elements with new moral pronouncements of their own—is the dominant theme of the nineteen centuries of history over which, in this highly schematic presentation, I propose to pass in a single paragraph. We will content ourselves with a bare list of important topics which would figure in a history of social thought during these centuries.

First, there would be the story of the failing impetus of Greek philosophy; then the story of Jewish prophecy and the origins of Christianity; the rise of Rome and of the Roman Empire and the elaboration of Roman Law and administration;

45

the Christianization and decline of the Roman Empire; the rise of Islam; the nadir of the Christian west; the medieval revival of Europe; the theological and philosophical debate of the middle ages; the establishment of universities; the humanistic renaissance; the protestant reformation; the precursors and pioneers of natural science; the development of technologies; the increase in trade and in the wealth of nations; the growth of cities and of populations.

These topics form part of our basic general knowledge of the history of our own antecedents in the west and this knowledge will be assumed here. I am concerned only to point out the major turning-points in the development of social eidos and in my scheme there are only two such turning-points. The first I have attributed to the Teachers of the First Millennium. The second is bound up with the rising power and prestige of the natural sciences and the scientific method. The origins of modern science can be traced back for centuries, but it is in the seventeenth century that science first stakes its claim to central importance. 'The seventeenth century did not merely bring a new factor into history, in the way we often assume—one that must just be added, so to speak, to the other permanent factors. The new factor immediately began to elbow at the other ones, pushing them out of their places—and, indeed, began immediately to seek control of the rest.'[1]

Applied natural science has been enormously potent in transforming the relationship between human societies and their natural environment; their populations have rapidly increased in numbers, they have produced and consumed more and more per head, and they have developed forms of political and economic organization geared to the developing exploitation of natural resources. Once the problem of controlling nature was seen to be technical, all other problems began to be treated as technical also. Right at the beginning of this process, before the actual achievements of science were very great, the

[1] H. Butterfield, *The Origins of Modern Science, 1300-1800*, p. 173.

ideological spokesmen of the new eidos, Bacon and Descartes, were predicting for scientific rationality an immediate, revolutionary breakthrough. 'They tended to believe that the scientific revolution could be carried out entirely in a single life-time. It was a question of changing one lantern-slide of the universe for another, in their opinion—establishing a new system to take the place of Aristotle's. Gradually they found that it would need not merely one generation but perhaps two to complete the task. By the close of the seventeenth century they had come to see that they had opened the way to an indefinitely expanding future, and that the sciences were only in their cradle still.'[1]

Here was put forward a programme for change in the eidos of natural philosophy with immense practical and social implications. While the early scientists themselves often were of a mystical frame of mind, with a predominantly religious motivation, those who popularized the idea of science associated it with far-reaching scepticism about all kinds of orthodoxy, political, religious and so on. In this sense there came into being with science itself an ideology of science manifesting itself, from the first, in social and economic theories. Thus the seventeenth century is a turning point not only of eidos in a general sense, but of social eidos in particular. 'The discoveries of seventeenth-century science were translated into a new outlook and a new world-view, not by scientists themselves, but by the heirs and successors of Fontenelle.'[2]

After the first steps towards 'a new world-view' had been taken, it was possible for philosophers and literary men (Locke in England and Voltaire in France, for example) to set the rational tone of eighteenth-century Enlightenment. But these first steps themselves required a hardihood of mind more

[1] *Ibid.* p. 83.

[2] *Ibid.*, p. 157. Fontenelle, secretary of the Académie des Sciences from 1699 to 1741, and a pioneer of scientific popularization, was an advocate, like his friend the Abbé de Saint-Pierre, of 'scientific politics.'

visionary than that of simple rationality. 'The teaching of Copernicus' writes Butterfield 'is entangled . . . with concepts of value, theological explanations and forms of what we should call animism.'[1] He 'rises to lyricism and almost to worship when he writes about the regal nature and the central position of the sun. He would not stand alone if he proved to have been stimulated by something like mysticism or neo-platonic sentiment'.[2] Kepler 'even more than Copernicus . . . was driven by a mystical semi-religious fervour—a passion to uncover the magic of mere numbers and to demonstrate the music of the spheres'.[3] Newton was even prepared to believe that gravity, which was otherwise so apparently unaccountable, represented the constant activity of a living being that pervaded the whole of space. We may compare Needham: 'Even the early Royal Society found it difficult to distinguish between science and what we should now call magic. In the sixteenth century science was commonly called "Natural Magic". Kepler was active as an astrologer and even Newton has with justice been called "the last of the magicians".'[4]

Especially in its early stages, the developers of the natural sciences needed audacious imagination. They were, after all, dealing in cosmic matters and with mysteries. The serious outlook of religious puritanism seems to have conduced to these investigations, which were conceived of as being to the greater glory of God as well as to the greater good of man. This affinity, suggested by Max Weber, was ably elaborated by Robert Merton in an important essay on 'Science, technology and society in seventeeth-century England'.[5]

The connection between science and the puritan ethic has been overstressed in more recent discussion, to the exclusion of

[1] *Ibid.*, p. 30.   [2] *Ibid.*, p. 24.   [3] *Ibid.*, p. 56.
[4] J. Needham, *Science and Civilization in China*, vol. II, p. 34. The last phrase is from J. M. Keynes's essay on 'Newton the Man'.
[5] First published in *Osiris*, IV.2, 1938, and, in shortened form, as Chap. XVIII of *Social Theory and Social Structure*, Revised Edition, 1957.

other connections equally worth considering.[1] The connection with magic, alchemy and astrology, for example, can be linked, in terms of imaginative sensibility, with tendencies, in poetry and the arts, towards daring metaphor and images of transmutation and metamorphosis. This tendency helps to explain some of the fanciful and even playful theories and experiments of the period, but there was also a growing sense of the concrete, material nature of phenomena, and this was directly bound up with growing technological control. And, perhaps most important of all, there was the rapid development of quantification and mathematical rationality.

In the first age of science, the sense of wonder remained strong and fresh. In the eighteenth century the trend was more prosaic, sceptical and utilitarian. The more prosaic and the more poetic aspects of the scientific eidos have both been apparent ever since, though the latter have continually had to yield ground. Gaston Bachelard has suggested that first developments in the sciences may always or often arise from unconscious fantasy, or from a level of thought where myth and metaphor are paramount.[2] But he also points out that science must always move further away from these origins.

The relation between the eidos of natural science and social eidos needs to be carefully considered. In the first place, there can be no serious question about the emergence, over the past three centuries, of a change in social eidos associated with the development of the natural sciences. By now this change has to some extent entered into the outlook of every person with even minimal education, on a world-wide scale. This is far from saying that everyone now thinks like a scientist about social questions. The influence of science on the thinking of ordinary men and women has been indirect. It stems partly, as Pareto pointed out, from 'the enormous development of industrial life,

[1] See B. Barber, 'Sociology of Science: a trend report and bibliography', *Current Sociology*, vol. V, No. 2, 1956.
[2] G. Bachelard, *La Formation de l'Esprit Scientifique*.

which is to a large extent an experimental life'.[1] This has had the effect of weakening the hold of older superstitions though in the name of science new superstitions have been introduced. The other effect has been through the development by intellectuals of rationalistic social theories which have become widely diffused, the idea of progress for example.

In the course of the eighteenth century the view began to gain ground among the intellectually inclined that, with the development of science and science-oriented thought, human history had entered a new political phase. It was felt that the political realities of the *ancien régime* had been concealed first of all by the dominant religious orthodoxies and then by 'metaphysic' which was merely the attempt to fill by words the vacuum which religion had left. The important idea of the 'stages of thought', and their association with successive stages of political development, has been traced to the early writings of Turgot (1727–81). From him by one route or another it reached Saint-Simon (1760–1825) and Comte (1798–1857), for both of whom it can plausibly be claimed that they explicitly stated a 'Law of the Three Stages' and that they linked the Third Stage with the emergence of a new 'positive science of man'.[2] Comte's formulation of the Law was 'that each of our leading conceptions,—each branch of our knowledge,—passes successively through three different theoretical conditions: the Theological, or fictitious; the Metaphysical, or abstract; and the Scientific, or positive. In other words, the human mind, by its nature, employs in its progress three methods of philosophizing, the character of which is essentially different, and even radically opposed: viz., the theological method, the metaphysical and the positive. Hence arise three philosophies, or general systems of conceptions on the aggregate of phenomena, each of which excludes the others. The first is the neces-

[1] V. Pareto, *The Mind and Society*, § 984.
[2] See E. Gouhier, *La Jeunesse d'Auguste Comte*, for documentation on the relationship of Comte to Saint-Simon.

sary point of departure of the human understanding; and the third is its fixed and definite state. The second is merely a state of transition'.[1]

This formulation, and its claim to be regarded as a law, has long fallen out of favour among philosophers and social scientists. Yet alike among professionals and laymen, the idea of historical stages of thought has in fact become a basic assumption of social eidos. On the one hand we may agree with the critics of positivism[2] that it was seriously misleading to represent the study of society as about to advance into 'its fixed and definitive state'. But on the other hand we may still consider that a distinctive 'third stage' of social eidos has resulted from the high prestige of science itself.[3]

[1] A. Comte, *The Positive Philosophy* (tr. Harriet Martineau), vol. I, p. 2.

[2] See, for instance, K. Popper, *The Poverty of Historicism* and F. A. Hayek, *The Counter-revolution of Science*.

[3] The presentation of the 'stages' in this book differs from that of Comte in a number of ways. Comte calls his first stage 'theological' and sub-divides it into (i) primitive fetichism (ii) polytheism and (iii) monotheism. His theological stage begins to disintegrate, and to give way to the transitional 'metaphysical' stage, at the beginning of the fourteenth century. The metaphysical stage is sub-divided into (i) the rise of the ideas of protestantism in the fourteenth and fifteenth centuries (ii) the development of the 'provisional philosophy', substantially completed in the seventeenth century by such thinkers as Hobbes, Spinoza and Bayle, and transmitted by Voltaire and the Encyclopaedists to a wide public during the eighteenth century.

The stage described in my chapter on 'Archaic Thought' corresponds to Comte's 'primitive fetichist' sub-stage combined with that part of his 'polytheist' sub-stage which precedes the rise of the Moral Teachers. My second stage is therefore much longer than his, covering the whole period from the rise of the Teachers in the First Millennium to the rise of the natural sciences in the seventeenth century. My third stage begins with that century, which is the beginning of the philosophical sub-stage of Comte's second stage.

Whereas the stages I have described are stages in the predominant social eidos, Comte is tracing the development of *all* branches of knowledge through his three stages. Some branches of knowledge, mathematics and astronomy for example, began to move into the positive stage long before it was possible for more complex subject-matters, such as those of biology and, most complex of all, sociology, to do so. The Greek philosophers had

51

established a 'great division' between 'the philosophy of the inorganic world, and that of moral and social man'. This 'was the first logical condition of all future progress, because it permitted the independent growth of inorganic philosophy (then in the metaphysical stage), whose more simple speculations might be rapidly perfected without injury to the social operation of moral philosophy (then in its theological stage), which was much less occupied with the abstract improvement of its doctrines, than with trying the fitness of theological conceptions for civilizing mankind. A rivalry, extending from doctrines to persons, immediately grew up between the metaphysical spirit, which was in possession of the scientific domain, and the theological, which governed morals: and it was the social ascendancy of moral philosophy which kept down intellectual enterprise in the direction of natural philosophy, and was the first cause of the retardation of science'. (*Positive Philosophy*, vol. II, p. 300.)

As Comte saw it, in the seventeenth century, natural philosophy moved from the metaphysical to the positive stage, while at the same time, moral philosophy moved from the theological to the metaphysical stage. It was his aim to bring moral philosophy to the same positive, scientific stage as that already attained by natural philosophy.

Comte took a moralistic view of the functions of science and sociology. This view and some of its more recent manifestations are criticized in the final chapter of this book. The second stage of social eidos, as I see it, is the stage of moral doctrine as a whole, whereas to Comte it is the relatively brief transition of morality from a theological to a scientific basis. The difference between the 'stages' presented here and those of Comte is thus seen to be something more than a matter of chronological adjustment.

PART II

Rationality in Social Eidos

Chapter 1

RATIONAL-TECHNICAL SOCIAL
EIDOS

At the archaic stage the picture of society was essentially mysterious and in the intervening stage it has been essentially moral and religious. At the contemporary stage, along with a plentiful inheritance of mystery and morality, there is an overriding tendency to look on society as a working system, which can be made to work better and better by rational-technical means. Central to this conception are first, the idea of progress, second, the economics of the market and third, the politics of the ballot box.

Historians of social thought have often described the rise to prominence and subsequent vicissitudes of the idea of progress. In its fully-fledged form, progress is conceived of as a general historical tendency, not only in increasing scientific knowledge and technical efficiency, but also in improving public and private morality, artistic achievement and 'happiness'. The main opposition to the idea has been due to misgivings about these latter areas of progress. There is no doubt, by now, about the empirical facts of technological advance.

Critics of the comprehensive idea of progress question whether non-material advance can be 'measured' in the same sense as mental advance, often indicating their own preference for the values of say, fifth-century Athens or the High Middle Ages over those of our own industrial epoch. Critics of these critics have sometimes viewed this lack of confidence in the

55

present and future as an ideology of reactionary nostalgia. The important point to note empirically, however, is the dominance in mass politics of the ideology of progress, whatever the misgivings of certain groups of intellectuals.

That this should be so is bound up with the political and economic organization of our epoch. Increasing scientific knowledge and technical efficiency has led to greater material productivity, the lengthening of life, the growth of population, the spread of education and the raising of levels of aspiration. Money and the market have provided the basic instrument for this development, and economic institutions have themselves been developed and refined for this end. The claim of larger and larger sections of the population to a share in the benefits of material advance has had to be repressed or diverted, or met by revolutionary or evolutionary means—in one way or another, it is a claim which has called for continuous political management. The basic instrument for this management has been the vote, as a means of legitimizing a given distribution of benefits or a given strategy of redistribution where this was required.

Of money and the vote we may say that if they are imperfect instruments in a rational-technical sense, at least no alternative instruments are obviously better. They are therefore assumed, perhaps rightly, to be indispensible devices for the regulation of social life in our epoch. Rather than replace them, governments seek to offset their inconveniences, while at the same time maintaining public confidence in their basic validity and rationality. It is so important to preserve this confidence that there is an inherent pressure to overstate the rationality and understate the irrationality of these two basic instruments, money and the vote. Their acceptance is conceived as a precondition for progress, and the idea of progress is conceived as essential for their effective utilization. Money, the vote and the idea of progress are thus bound up with each other as the fundamentals of society in our epoch, and the perceiving of this is the essence of contemporary social eidos. We are not concerned here with the accuracy of this perception, only with its universality. It is not, of course, an explicit part of general social indoctrination in so highly simplified a form. The ordinary child or man meets it as it is expressed in the actual functioning of the complicated institutions with which he has dealings and also in the ideologies that go with these institutions. Every economic and political institution has its associated ideological validation. Ultimately these validations are linked with the relatively abstract supra-ideological systems of economic and political theory.

The point to be emphasized in this brief analysis is the pressure which exists in modern society towards a belief in the technical-rational validity of the basic economic and political instruments as social regulators. They are conceived as the rational means towards progress. Behind this conception are two assumptions that are absolutely fundamental, firstly the assumption that rationality is what is to be aimed at and secondly the assumption that rationality is virtually the same as rational-technicality, i.e. the expert and efficient use of means.

Whether rationality can in fact mean anything different from this is a philosophical and psychological question. If philosophers or psychologists were able to establish another meaning, and if this meaning was generally accepted, this would lead on to a major transformation of social eidos. Such a transformation is difficult to imagine, but it is possible, and the possibility is worth considering. It is possible, in other words, that the three stages we looked at in the three previous chapters are the precursors of a fourth stage. There are certainly contradictions within the third stage, but whether they represent the surviving influence of the first and second stages or a premonition of a further stage, it is singularly hard to tell. We are ill equipped with concepts and with methods for investigating these alternatives.

The position stated rather baldly in this chapter forms, as I see it, a necessary bridge between the opening chapters and the rest of the book, where I consider some of the theories about the nature of society and social eidos, from Comte onwards, which might conceivably have relevance for a future reconstruction, both of society and of social eidos.

These theories constitute, to my mind, the inner conceptual core of the 'new' intellectual discipline of sociology. To change the metaphor, the sociological theorist of the nineteenth and early twentieth century seems to me like a man, with one foot still stuck in the moralistic past, attempting to arrive at one stride at the goal of a science of politics, and dimly discerning, as he struggles to free himself for this advance, the limitations in this context of the eidos of the natural sciences, and the strange inter-mixture of freedom and compulsion in all human and all social thought. Comte was the most dogmatic in stating the finality of the positive stage of social thought, and, paradoxically, the most involved in the earlier, moralistic stage. Marx, although he never fully worked out or stated his sociology, has helped a later age to realize the pervasiveness of ideology in all social theory. Pareto, less politically committed and more generally sceptical, took this realization a stage further and pointed to some of the mysterious underlying compulsions in social thinking and behaving. Freud was a pioneer in the analysis of these compulsions in terms of human biology and psychological development. These new elements in the theoretical self-consciousness of the sociologist remain confused and unassimilated even in the sphere of the professional social sciences, while in the wider sphere of lay thinking the process of clarification has barely begun. Our institutions and our ideas about them are essentially based on concepts originating in the eighteenth and early nineteenth centuries.

Sociologists, besides analysing social eidos, have begun to contribute to the social eidos of the layman. We are concerned with them in both capacities. The main concern in the pages that follow, however, is with the broad outline of the contribution of Comte, Marx, Pareto, Freud (and the Parsonian 'synthesis') to the theory of ideology, or, to describe it in another way, to the critical analysis of social rationalization.

Chapter 2

COMTE, MARX AND THE THEORY OF IDEOLOGY

It is instructive to compare and contrast the historical background and influence of Comte and Marx. Both had every intention of exercising a decisive influence through their ideas. Both lacked scientific modesty though they claimed scientific status. Both greatly over-estimated (at any rate in the earlier part of their careers) the speed with which their ideas would be accepted and changes would be brought about. Both left a formidable legacy.

Comte was born twenty years earlier than Marx and he was brought up in the aftermath of the French revolution which seemed to him by far the most outstanding event in history up to that date. For him, therefore, the revolution was over: for Marx, however, it had not taken place. Hence we find Comte writing in an early essay (1822) called 'Plan of the scientific operations necessary for reorganizing society':

'The fundamental datum and positive starting point of general practical politics consists . . . in a determination of the real tendency of civilization. By ascertaining this we can harmonize political action with it and render as mild, and as short as possible the crisis which the human race inevitably undergoes during its successive passages through the different stages of civilization.'[1]

Like Saint-Simon, Comte believed that scientists, including

[1] The essay appears as an appendix to *Positive Polity*, vol. IV, p. 562.

social scientists, were about to become the spiritual leaders of mankind, while the executive functions of Government would be carried on by businessmen and bankers. When Marx wrote of Comtean positivism as 'rot',[1] it was probably because Comte was in favour of a gradual, scientific re-education of *all* classes, whereas to Marx the future leadership of society lay with an organized working class.[2]

It is necessary however to note that Comte, like Marx, was deeply indignant about the social irresponsibility of industrial capitalism. Also, like Marx, he was a determined and uncompromising atheist. A few quotations will illustrate this. Thus Comte wrote to his friend Valat in 1819:

'My friend, this class of hard-working, open, estimable, men whom we both love, is oppressed and ignobly exploited by its superiors. The fruit of its toil should belong to it entirely. It should cease to nourish the infamous luxury and base idleness of its masters. Social order, now organized for the benefit of the useless people, should be organized solely for the useful. Here, friend, lies our duty—you and I, who spring from the oppressed class, and who can help a little, according to our lights and our abilities, must aid in realizing this great change.'[3]

At the time of the revolution of 1830, Comte was notified of his enrolment in the counter-revolutionary National Guard. He declined: 'Being republican by sympathy and conviction I am not going to swear that, at the peril of my life and that of others, I will defend a Government which, if I were a man of action, I should fight against.'[4] In 1848, he took no part in the revolution of February; but in March he founded the Positivist Society. In July he wrote: 'There are now but two camps—the camp of reaction and anarchy, which acknowledges more

[1] In a letter to Engels in 1866.
[2] It is odd that Marxists should have forgiven exactly this notion in Saint-Simon, but not in Comte. See F. Engels, *Socialism Utopian and Scientific*, p. 12.
[3] Letter to Valat, 24 September 1819.
[4] Quoted by E. Littré, *Auguste Comte et la Philosophie Positive*, p. 252.

or less distinctly the direction of God; the camp of construction and progress, which is wholly devoted to Humanity.'[1]

In his *System of Positive Polity*, Comte explains why 'it is among the working classes that the new philosophers' (i.e. the scientifically trained, sociologically oriented intelligentsia) 'will find their most energetic allies'.[2] For, he writes, 'the philosopher is, under certain aspects, a member of the working class fully trained; while the working man is in many respects a philosopher without the training. Both too will look with similar feelings upon the intermediate or capitalist class'.[3]

Capitalists have mediocre moral status: 'The principal condition for (practical success) is the combination of a certain amount of energy with great caution, and a fair amount of perseverance. . . . Vigorous exertion of the active powers is more frequently induced by the personal propensities of avarice, ambition or vanity, than by the higher instincts.'[4] The workmen, especially in Paris, are morally superior: 'Their personal experience of the miseries of life is a constant stimulus to the nobler sympathies.'[5] 'Positivism rejects the metaphysical doctrine of the sovereignty of the people.'[6] But: 'The dictatorship which our transitional policy requires, as long as the spiritual interregnum lasts, must arise in the first instance from their ranks. . . . On historical grounds I feel convinced that the workmen of France are more likely than any other class to supply men competent for supreme power.'[7]

Comte went a long way here towards the Marxist conception of proletarian dictatorship, though he looked on political Communism as an ideological aberration. All the same, 'To do justice to Communism, we must look at the generous sym-

[1] A. Comte, *General View of Positivism*.

[2] *System of Positive Polity*, vol. I, Chap. III, 'The Action of Positivism upon the Working Classes'.

[3] *Ibid.*, p. 103.   [4] *Ibid.*, p. 104.

[5] *Ibid.*, p. 105. One may note that Comte's estimate on this point is at variance with the contemporary observation of Le Play on working class family morality in Paris.   [6] *Ibid.*, p. 106.   [7] *Ibid.*, p. 160.

pathies by which it is inspired, not at the shallow theories in which those sympathies find expression provisionally, until circumstances enable them to take some other shape. The workmen connected with the Communist utopia, caring but very little for metaphysical principles, do not attach nearly the same importance to these theories as is done by men of literary education'.[1]

Laissez faire, he wrote, as an economic policy was to be rejected in favour of planning: 'Nothing can excuse the metaphysical school of economics for systematically resisting the intervention of human wisdom in the various departments of social action.'[2] He envisaged workers' organizations: 'When French workmen are allowed to concert their plans as freely as their employers, the antagonism of interests that will then arise will make both sides feel the need of a moral power to arbitrate between them.'[3] On the other hand in another part of the *Positive Polity*, he wrote on the errors of socialism, which he described as 'industrial demagogism' and as 'even more ephemeral than national industrialism'.[4] Education by the positivist 'priesthood' was to make each class contented with its lot. 'It is in the proletary class especially that the priesthood will repress ambition, for in that class it is as fatal to happiness as to duty, allowing for cases of an exceptional aptitude for the patriciate.'[5] Comte had a lifelong distaste for newspapers which he avoided for reasons of 'cerebral hygiene'. Consequently, the positive polity, while allowing freedom of the press, would dispense with newspapers: 'A judicious use of placards, with the addition of a few occasional pamphlets— this is all Positivism requires to regenerate public opinion.'[6]

These quotations illustrate some interesting resemblances and differences between Comte and Marx. In the revolution of 1848 the middle-aged Comte went through the same historical experiences as the young Marx; in some ways, their reading of

[1] *Ibid.*, p. 121.   [2] *Ibid.*, p. 124.   [3] *Ibid.*, p. 134.
[4] *Ibid.*, p. 284.   [5] *Ibid.*, p. 290.   [6] *Ibid.*, p. 332.

the situation was remarkably similar. But there remained the all-important difference that while Marx was never tired of stressing the unity of theory and practice, Comte advocated a division of labour between the theorists (i.e. sociologists, scientific educators, and priests of the religion of humanity) and the practical politicians who were also to be the managers of industry and finance. As early as 1821, he wrote to Valat: 'I am working to establish doctrines, not institutions. When the former take shape, that is to say in about sixty years time, we can think about the latter. . . . I am not exactly saying "my kingdom is not of this world" but the equivalent in terms of our epoch.'[1] Marx, on the contrary, looked on this kind of separation of function as a bourgeois device to sustain what he called the 'false consciousness' of society. His party leaders had to be intellectuals and his intellectuals had to take part in the hurly-burly of political life.

In his treatment of the problem of ideology, Marx did not imply that ideas were unimportant. It was a blockage in the realm of ideas which prevented men from taking the action necessary to bring the social order into line with changed economic conditions. Ideas were being used, consciously and unconsciously, to maintain an outdated *status quo*, and these ideas, which constituted the 'false consciousness' of the epoch, had to be combated and exposed, and replaced by others more in tune with reality. But he insisted that so long as this 'battle of ideas' was carried on at a purely theoretical level, among the intellectuals themselves, it would fail to resolve the confusion and in fact would only add to it. The mass of the people would remain unaffected by the wrangling of the intellectuals; and the intellectuals themselves, by isolating themselves from the masses and from the political struggle, would lack the touchstone of reality against which to test the meaningfulness or otherwise of their verbal disputation.

Marx saw that he had to do battle not only with the ruling

[1] Quoted by E. Gouhier, *La Jeunesse d'Auguste Comte*, vol. III, p. 334.

class but with the tendency in the intellectuals to avoid the harshness of politics, the crassness of economics. This gave a peculiar double edge to his pronouncements on ideology.[1] He and Engels devoted much of their literary output to involved polemics with intellectual opponents of whom few still evoke our interest. It was on this anvil that they forged the angry and intolerant idiom of communist discussion, an idiom which was forcefully revived by Lenin when he came to argue out the Bolshevik party line. One may regret this pugnacious tone, especially when it is applied by later Marxists to wholesale condemnation of non-Marxist thought and scholarship; to understand it more fully one has to transpose oneself into the mood of the polemical works of 1845–7, especially *The German Ideology*. In the preface to this work, Marx wrote that its aim was 'to discredit the philosophic struggle with the shadows of reality, which appeals to the dreamy and muddled German nation'.[2] Especially in the first part, (rather misleadingly entitled 'Feuerbach'), Marx and Engels elucidate their general theory of ideology in several important passages:

'The ideas of the ruling class are in every epoch the ruling ideas: i.e. the class, which is the ruling material force of society, is at the same time its ruling intellectual force. The class which has the means of material production at its disposal has control at the same time over the means of mental production, so that

[1] The term 'ideology' was first used by the French philosopher Destutt de Tracy in his book, *Elements of Ideology* (1801–15), to describe a possible science of human ideas. He and his group criticized Napoleon who in turn attacked them in a speech in 1812, in which he contrasted the 'dark metaphysic' of ideology with the 'knowledge of the heart and the lessons of history.' The terms 'ideology' and 'ideologist' thenceforward took on a derogatory meaning. In 1819, in an early article, Comte criticized de Tracy for 'wanting to deduce the fundamental principles of politics from ideological analyses' and he called this 'pure metaphysic'. (Quoted by Gouhier, *op. cit.*, vol. III, p. 291.) One can see here the beginning of a pattern in which different groups accuse each other of particular varieties of intellectualist delusion, even though each group had come into existence on a programme of ending such delusion.

[2] K. Marx and F. Engels. *The German Ideology*. Tr. Roy Pascall, p. 2.

thereby, generally speaking, the ideas of those who lack the means of mental production are subject to it. The ruling ideas are nothing more than the ideal expression of the dominant material relationships, the dominant material relationships expressed as ideas; hence of the relationships which make the one class the ruling one, therefore the ideas of its dominance. The individuals composing the ruling class possess among other things consciousness, and therefore think. In so far, therefore, as they rule as a class and determine the extent and compass of an epoch, it is self-evident that they do this in their whole range, hence among other things rule also as thinkers, as producers of ideas, and regulate the production and distribution of the ideas of their age: thus their ideas are the ruling ideas of the epoch. For instance, in an age and in a country where royal power, aristocracy and bourgeoisie are contending for mastery and where, therefore, mastery is shared, the doctrine of the separation of powers proves to be the dominant idea and is expressed as an "eternal law".'[1]

The model put forward here is of a society with a single ruling class and its associated ideology, but in the last sentence this is elaborated into a more complex model where 'mastery is shared', and ideology is brought in to validate, or legitimate, this balancing of power. There is a further interesting complication:

'The division of labour, which we saw above as one of the chief forces of history up till now, manifests itself also in the ruling class as the division of mental and material labour, so that inside this class one part appears as the thinkers of the class (its active, conceptive ideologists, who make the perfecting of the illusion of the class about itself their chief source of livelihood), while the others' attitude to these ideas and illusions is more passive and receptive, because they are in reality the active members of this class and have less time to make up ideas and illusions about themselves. Within this class this

[1] *Ibid.*, p. 39.

cleavage can even develop into a certain opposition and hostility between the two parts, which, however, in the case of a practical collision, in which the class itself is endangered, automatically comes to nothing.'[1]

In other words, the theoreticians of society, whose general function is to bolster it up, may on occasion criticize it but remain too loyal to the *status quo* to push their criticism very far. If their criticism becomes serious this 'presupposes the existence of a revolutionary class'. Such a class, however will be:

'. . . . compelled, merely in order to carry through its aim, to represent its interest as the common interest of all the members of society, put in an ideal form; it will give its ideas the form of universality, and represent them as the only rational, universally valid ones. The class making a revolution appears from the very start, merely because it is opposed to a *class*, not as a class but as the representative of the whole of society; it appears as the whole mass of society confronting the one ruling class. It can do this because, to start with, its interest really is more connected with the common interest of all other non-ruling classes, because under the pressure of conditions its interest has not yet been able to develop as the particular interest of a particular class. Its victory, therefore, benefits also many individuals of the other classes which are not winning a dominant position, but only in so far as it now puts these individuals in a position to raise themselves into the ruling class. When the French bourgeoisie overthrew the power of the aristocracy, it thereby made it possible for many proletarians to raise themselves above the proletariat, but only in so far as they became bourgeois.'[1]

The next revolution, Marx and Engels thought, would bring into power the proletariat itself, and thereby class rule would come to an end with it 'this whole pretence, that the rule of a certain class is only the rule of certain ideas'.[2] The recent history of revolution appears to show, however, that though

---

[1] *Ibid.*, p. 40.
[2] *Ibid.*, p. 41. I have substituted the word 'pretence' for 'semblance'.

classes may support revolutions they do not gain power from them. There is a complex shift of power, but power itself can only be held by a small group of individuals who attain it by a variety of means. Even the bourgeoisie was too numerous a class ever to constitute a true 'ruling class'; the proletariat, far more numerous, has only ever 'ruled' in an ideological sense. None the less, the Marxian critique of the Young Hegelians has had one highly significant sequel; it has led to the development of the roles of 'party member' and 'party theoretician', professional ideologists, agitators, propagandists, intellectuals turned activists, subscribing to a political party which demands the selfless, dedicated allegiance in the past given only to a church or sect. It is obvious that such persons have played and are playing roles of crucial importance in revolutionary and post-revolutionary situations in great areas of the contemporary world.

The Marxian theory of ideology was not a completely worked out theory. If one seeks for relevant texts in the writings of Marx and Engels, they are few and far between. The 'theory' was left in a state which was more suitable for use in polemic than in rational analysis. It has however persisted both in its original form and as the starting point for much non-Marxist discussion of the part played by ideas in society.

The term ideology is often applied to the whole wide range of mental activities in society: 'the legal, political, religious, aesthetic or philosophic—in short, ideological forms in which men become conscious of . . . conflict and fight it out.'[1] At other times it is applied more narrowly to the 'dominant idea' of a particular 'ruling class': the rest of the 'ideological forms' are then subsidiary hangers on of the dominant idea. In either usage, one could perhaps paraphrase 'ideology' as meaning 'a set of principles allegedly validating a system of social institutions'. Such a paraphrase would emphasize the rationalizing component in the ideology. Historically, 'ideologies'

[1] K. Marx, *Preface to Critique of Political Economy.*

68

were identified as such at a period when rationalization was the order of the day, when politics were crystallizing on party lines with principles and theories as part of their equipment. For the sake of clarity, it might be preferable if the term 'ideology' could be reserved for a phenomenon which historically became significant at about the same time that the name was invented. It is a characteristic product of the third stage of social eidos. If we use it indiscriminately for all forms of mental activity, and for the characteristic mental activities of the first and second stages of social eidos, we tend to read into, say, totemism or early Christianity a rationalistic eidos which was foreign to these stages.

From the seventeenth century onwards, many philosophers were exposing religion as irrational and as lending support to an irrational and unjust form of social organization, and they proposed various forms of rationality in its stead. But these forms of rationality were in turn exposed by others as pseudo-rational, and were described by analogy as 'religious' or 'metaphysical'. The Young Hegelians specialized in this style of debunking.

'The entire body of German philosophical criticism from Strauss to Stirner is confined to criticism of religious conceptions. The critics started from real religion and actual theology. What religious consciousness and a religious conception really meant was determined variously as they went along. Their advance consisted in subsuming the allegedly dominant metaphysical, political, juridical, moral and other conceptions under the class of religious or theological conceptions; and similarly in pronouncing political, juridical, moral consciousness as religious or theological, and the political, juridical, moral man—"man" in the last resort—as religious. The dominance of religion was taken for granted. Gradually every dominant relationship was pronounced a religious relationship and transformed into a cult, a cult of law, cult of the State, etc. On all sides it was only a question of dogmas and belief in dogmas. The world was sanctified to an ever-increasing extent till at last our venerable Saint Max (Max Stirner) was able to canonize it *en bloc* and thus dispose of it once for all.'[1]

The Young Hegelians sought to debunk social institutions by describing them as 'religious'; Marx and Engels considered such debunking to be politically ineffective; so they described the Young Hegelians as 'ideologists', with its associated meaning 'misguided intellectuals'. But meantime they took over the term 'ideology' in an all-inclusive sense, as covering all sorts of manifestations, at the level of ideas, of relationships and conflicts which they regarded as basically economic. Failure to face up to the overriding importance of the economic base was stigmatized by them as a sign of political weakness and obscurantism, intentional or otherwise.

In sociology as it has developed in more recent times, the equivalent of the Marxist theory of ideology is the so-called 'sociology of knowledge':

'Marxist thought attached such decisive significance to political practice conjointly with the economic interpretation of events, that these two became the ultimate criteria for disentangling what is mere ideology from those elements in thought which are more immediately relevant to reality. Consequently it is no wonder that the conception of ideology is usually regarded as integral to, and even identified with, the Marxist proletarian movement.

'But in the course of more recent intellectual and social developments, however, this stage has already been passed. It is no longer the exclusive privilege of socialist thinkers to trace bourgeois thought to ideological foundations and thereby to discredit it. Nowadays groups of every standpoint use this weapon against all the rest.'[2]

Specifically, Mannheim suggested that it was the function of the intellectuals to see beyond the perspective of any parti-

[1] K. Marx and F. Engels, *The German Ideology*, p. 5.
[2] K. Mannheim, *Ideology and Utopia*, p. 66.

cular class, because they themselves were recruited from many classes and attached to none. They would thus be able to work towards a 'science of politics'. Examining the prospects, in 1929, for such a science, Mannheim concluded that it was definitely possible, though he thought that 'the intellectuals in the present epoch could not become independently politically active. In an epoch like our own, where class interests and positions are becoming more sharply defined and derive their force and direction from mass action, political conduct which seeks other means of support would scarcely be possible'.[1] Therefore he conceived of the intellectuals as playing the part of 'watchmen' rather than as taking part in the actual processes of political decision. 'A political sociology which aims not at inculcating a decision but prepares the way for arriving at decisions will be able to understand relationships in the political realm which have scarcely even been noticed before.'[2]

Such formulations would have seemed to Marx to be lacking in teeth. Even Comte would have found them singularly un-ambitious. This is a measure of the disillusionment, since their day, with the idea of social science, or rather the shedding of earlier illusions about it. Yet even so, in his approach to politics Mannheim went much further than most contemporary sociologists are prepared to go.[3]

[1] *Ibid.*, p. 143.   [2] *Ibid.*, p. 145.
[3] One is tempted to speculate that if *The German Ideology* were brought up to date, it would include instructive sections addressed not only to Karl Mannheim but also to his critic, Karl Popper.

Chapter 3

THE ANALYSIS OF THE IRRATIONAL:
PARETO AND FREUD

The general direction of thought that was favoured by the rise of the natural sciences and scientific technology was, as we have seen, to regard all problems, including social, political and economic problems, as soluble by technical-rational means. Yet there were strong resistances to this way of thinking, partly because social eidos had so long been dominated by the characteristic ideas of the first and second stages, partly perhaps because of some shortcoming in the technical-rational eidos when applied to human society. Because the resistances were associated with conservative social forces, the advocates of a technical-rational social eidos tended to be radical or revolutionary. The thinkers of the Enlightenment who provided the ideology of the French Revolution were in effect claiming that society should be reconstructed on a more rational, a more technically efficient basis than that of the *ancien régime*. A similar claim by Marx and the Marxists provided the ideology of the Russian and Chinese revolutions. Revolution was put forward as a rational-technical solution of the social problem. The positivist and sociological thinkers of the nineteenth century claimed that by sociological techniques it was possible to achieve a solution without disruptive revolutionary conflict. The common assumptions of all these thinkers were, first, that it was possible and desirable for society to be rationally organized; second, that even if there were important irrational elements in men's minds and in social institutions, these could be contained, controlled, guided and harnessed; and third, that a decisive break with past stages of social eidos was necessary and imminent.

Alternative positions developed. For those who held onto religious beliefs, it was possible to argue that these beliefs, too, were consistent with rationality, or else that the human mind and spirit could operate on a plane which transcended rationality. These two strains in Christian theology had already existed side by side for centuries. It was also possible to argue that some people, by temperament and education, were better able than others, who were in the majority, to be rational in their religion. The rational minority should therefore concede to the irrational majority its need for myths and symbols.[1] Furthermore, if this argument was valid for religion, it could be valid for the ordering of social matters. Social mythology could be seen as a necessary instrument for the ordering of society, whether this was conceived of as being in the interests of the members of society as a whole, or primarily of a ruling élite.

Towards the end of the nineteenth century, there arose in Europe a number of sociologists, philosophers and psychologists who, while largely independent of each other, appear to exemplify a significant general trend. Its direction is towards re-establishing, in one form or another, the importance of the 'non-rational' (more explicitly, of the non-technical-rational) as an element of social eidos.[2] It was claimed by the American sociologist Parsons, for example, in his influential study, *The Structure of Social Action* (1937), that he could demonstrate a convergence in the conceptual systems developed by Pareto in Italy, Durkheim in France and Max Weber in Germany, and

[1] Compare Burckhardt's dictum on nineteenth-century religion, that it was 'rationalism for the few and magic for the many'. Quoted by E. R. Dodds, *The Greeks and the Irrational*, p. 192.

[2] For the historical background, see H. Stuart Hughes, *Consciousness and Society—the Orientation of European Social Thought, 1890-1930*.

that the analytical position arrived at independently by these three is in fact fundamental for a valid sociological theory. In the preface to the Second Edition (1949), Parsons wrote that he now realized that Freud was at least equally important in 'the same general movement of thought.' In his own later writings he has sought to combine Freudian concepts with those which, on his interpretation, emerged from the work of Pareto, Durkheim and Weber. The reader who is interested in Parsons will find in the next chapter a discussion of his views in relation to the current re-appraisal of the central concepts of social eidos. I wish, however, to emphasize in particular the contribution of Pareto and to link it with the sociological speculations in the later writings of Freud.

Vilfredo Pareto (1848–1923), engineer, economist and sociologist, wrote at the end of his life a long and important book, first published in 1916 as *Trattato di Sociologia generale*, translated by Arthur Livingston under the title *The Mind and Society* (1935). In this his last work he attempted to classify and analyse the non-logical elements in social thought. He takes his examples from literature, history and the events of his own time. His work is based on the library rather than on direct observation. But it constitutes a unique attempt at a comprehensive, systematic taxonomy of the varieties of human non-logicality in relation to social behaviour.

Pareto wrote in a mood of reaction against humanitarianism and assumptions about human progress and increasing rationality. He is strongly critical of positivist optimism and the claims of social doctrine to scientific status. None the less, he expresses sympathy with the Marxist position in so far as this seeks to expose the part played by class interests in forming ideologies. Though in general critical of most of his contemporaries, he is consistently respectful to Sorel, the syndicalist philosopher who thought that a socialist revolution might be brought about by the deliberate cultivation of social myths.[1]

[1] See, for example, V. Pareto, *The Mind and Society*, § 1868.

Though describing Socialism as a 'religion', Pareto writes that 'it is a great school of discipline, and one may even go so far as to say that, from that standpoint, it runs a close second to Catholicism. Better than any legislative enactment—not excepting compulsory education—it has succeeded in raising the molecules in an amorphous mass of humanity to dignified status as citizens, and in so doing it has increased the capacities for action of society as a whole'.[1] Describing the class conflict of the nineteenth century, he writes: 'From the working-men's side came a flood of subtle theories that were agitated by "intellectuals" and accepted by the working-people in blind faith and without any comprehension of them. . . . But disregarding their fatuity as arguments and looking only at their substance, one soon observes that it has been to the advantage of the working-classes to aim, in that fashion, at fantastic ideals; for, in virtue of the stubborn battle that they have fought for them and which they might perhaps not have fought under any other inspiration, and thanks to valiant aid from the allies whom they have recruited through the ideal character of their purposes, the working-classes have managed to improve their lot very appreciably in the course of the nineteenth century. As regards a nation or society as a whole, it is much more difficult to decide whether or not that change has been for the better. An affirmative answer would seem to be the more probable.'[2]

I present these quotations at the outset because Pareto has been associated in many people's minds with fascist politics. He has been as unfortunate in his friends as in his critics. This may be one explanation for his neglect in recent years, and for the fact that it is his theory of circulation of the élite, with its pessimistic implications, which is usually stressed by those who mention him. Parsons' three chapters on Pareto in *The Structure of Social Action* are commendably fair-minded and he notes that: 'Persons of liberal antecedents are often impressed,

[1] *Ibid.*, § 1858.   [2] *Ibid.*, § 1884, footnote.

THE ANALYSIS OF THE IRRATIONAL:

perhaps more strongly than in any other way, by a kind of Machiavellian element in Pareto's thought. This takes the form of laying great emphasis on the social importance of force and fraud.'[1] Moreover he 'was particularly pessimistic about the immediate outlook for liberal civilization in Europe. This is an Old World pessimism which it is difficult for Americans to understand. One possible reason for the prevailing hostility to Pareto in this country is that he was a "knocker" not a "booster".'[2]

This is not Pareto's only drawback. There is some inconsistency in his use of certain key terms in his system, namely those with a psychological reference. This is mainly I think because he did not regard it as within his competence to supply a psychological foundation for his sociological theory. There is no direct reference in his work to the ideas of Freud, relevant as these must seem to us now. The psychological terms Pareto used were meant to be provisional only. In view of rapid changes in psychology, still taking place, it may prove an advantage in some ways that Pareto focused attention on socially manifested forms of thinking and behaving, rather than attempting to explore the human mind in depth.

Pareto's central thesis is that a great deal of social behaviour is connected in its motivation with certain elements in man's thought which he calls *residues*.[3] The explanations that men give for what they do vary much more than do their actual patterns of behaviour. These explanations he calls *derivations* and they 'derive' from the underlying residues. The derivations are highly variable, while the residues are relatively constant.

---

[1] Parsons, *The Structure of Social Action*, p. 289.   [2] *Ibid.*, p. 293

[3] He insists (*ibid.*, § 868) that 'nothing, absolutely nothing is to be inferred from the proper meanings' of this or any other of his terms or their etymologies. Residues might equally well be called X-elements, or anything else. His translator none the less points out in a footnote that 'Etymologically, a "residue" would be "what is kept" (the constant element) when the variable elements have been eliminated from an action or reasoning by a comparative analysis.'

76

The derivations can be regarded as a secondary product of human activity, stemming from the 'hunger for logical explanation' which Pareto regards as one of the persistent, built-in elements of human social thought.

'The animal does not reason, it acts exclusively by instinct. It uses no derivations therefore. The human being, however, wants to think and he also feels impelled to keep his instincts and sentiments hidden from view. Rarely, in consequence, is at least a germ of derivation missing in human thinking, just as residues are rarely missing. Residues and derivations can be detected every time we look at a theory or argument that is not strictly logico-experimental.'[1]

Pareto uses the term *instinct* in the ordinary sense as meaning an innate response to a given set of stimuli by a given pattern of behaviour, as opposed to a culturally induced pattern. The term *sentiment* he uses somewhat more ambiguously to include both innate patterns of feeling and response and, more generally, the more emotional, less rational elements in the mind—elements which, he suggests, may be partly 'hidden from view', that is to say unconscious or incompletely conscious. Psychologists have used the term sentiment to describe specific socially induced feelings and attachments, such as patriotism, but I do not myself think that Pareto intended to give it this meaning. Unfortunately he has left a certain ambiguity as to the relation of sentiment to residue. In some passages he uses these terms as though they were interchangeable. Elsewhere[2] he writes that the residues are manifestations of sentiments. I think this is probably his more considered usage, and that while sentiments are feelings pure and simple, residues are suffused with emotion but are also partly cognitive or pseudo-cognitive. They are 'the principles underlying non-logical actions'.[3] The residue 'exists in the mind of the human being'.[4] Although it is not logical,

---

[1] *Ibid.*, § 1400.   [2] For example § 1401.
[3] § 306. A footnote explains that 'principle' here means simply 'the cause to which an action is to be ascribed'.   [4] § 798.

it can be rationalized by pseudo-logical explanation, or 'derivation'. It *feels* as though it were logical. At the extreme furthest from logico-experimental science, 'there are cases in which the logical inference is not clearly manifested, as in what jurists call 'latent principles in law'. Psychologists explain such phenomena as effects of the subconscious or in some other way. We do not choose to go so far back here; we stop at the fact, leaving the explanation of it to others.'[1]

In spite of this ambiguity in the definition of residues, their nature becomes clear from the many examples given in the course of the work. They are ways of thinking and modes of conduct which appear persistently in human social behaviour. In derivations, verbal expression is paramount. In residues, the verbal element is absent or subsidiary. Actions, rituals, prescribed relationships and implicit normative principles precede and are more permanent and less variable than the verbal explanations of them. The residue is an unformulated principle for action. Pareto says that it is the non-logical equivalent of an axiom or basic principle in 'logico-experimental science', the phrase by which he always refers to the natural sciences. In the sciences these axioms are duly formulated, but a residue *cannot* be logically formulated. Derivations, which have the appearance of formulating it, are logical in form only, that is, are pseudo-logical. This is to say that the residues are inadequately tested by the standards of testing normal to logico-experimental science. Yet, as underlying principles of social action, they are oriented towards objective reality. If, as principles, they are not 'proved', neither are they disproved. As Pareto points out, societies which act on them have survived and behaviour based on them has not therefore been incompatible with survival.

Residues are hypothetical elements in the human mind. They are assumed to be the constant, underlying elements which give rise to a multitude of variable derivations. These

[1] § 802.

derivations *are* directly observable. Pareto's procedure was to observe and collect a great many derivations and to classify them according to what, on his hypothesis, was the underlying, constant element, or residue, in each case.[1] As an example, he takes the Christian custom of baptism. It is known that there are many other customs of a similar kind.

'The pagans too had lustral water, and they used it for purposes of purification. If we stopped at that, we might associate the use of water with the fact of purification. But other cases of baptism show that the use of water is not a constant element. Blood may be used for purification, and other substances as well. Nor is that all: there are numbers of rites that effect the same result. In cases where taboos have been violated, certain rites remove the pollution that a person has incurred in one set of circumstances or another. So the circle of similar facts widens, and in the great variety of devices and in the many explanations that are given for their use the thing which remains constant is the feeling, the sentiment, that the integrity of an individual which has been altered by certain causes, real or imaginary, can be restored by certain rites. The given case, therefore, is made up of that constant element, a, and a variable element, b, the latter comprising the means that are used for restoring the individual's integrity and the reasonings by which the efficiency of the means is presumably explained. The human being has a vague feeling that water somehow cleanses moral as well as material pollutions. However, he does not, as a rule, justify his conduct in that manner. The explanation would be far too simple. So he goes looking for something more complicated, more pretentious, and readily finds what he is looking for.'[2]

Here Pareto, in taking an example from the religious ritual of his own society, and linking it with the sort of magical practices reported by travellers and ethnographers, is in a tradition which goes back to Fontenelle, and to Lucian before

[1] § 1402.　　　　　　　　　　　　　　　　　[2] § 863.

him. It is indeed likely that he was influenced by the writings of Sir James Frazer, who collected and classified numerous examples of primitive magical belief.[1] But it is worth noting that Pareto's data relate to *primitive* aspects of the behaviour of *civilized* peoples. He does not draw substantially, as Frazer did, on anthropological data. Moreover, he by no means confines himself to the recognized areas of religion and ritual. He finds 'religious' tendencies in areas commonly regarded as 'rational'. He writes of the 'religion of socialism' and the 'sex religion', meaning by the latter the crusade against sexual immorality which he regarded as hypocritical and irrational. Indeed he finds pseudo-logical reasoning dominant in the discussion of economic and political questions, and in the writings of sociologists themselves.

'From the Middle Ages on to our time, the influence of magic on human societies has lessened, even if we reckon in the count its legacies to mind-readings, spiritualisms, telepathies and other systems of thaumaturgy; but the domain from which it was banished has been partly occupied by the goddess Science. Taken all in all, in the departments of the arts and sciences development has certainly been in the direction of an increase in the importance attached to experimental methods; but the evidence in favour of such an increase is not so good if we turn to the fields of politics and social organization. It is significant that simple combinations foreign to scientific experience are far from having disappeared from modern social life; in fact, they persist in great numbers, thriving in prosperous exuberance.'[2]

Pareto, himself an economist, believed that economics was a genuine science, though equally he believed that by itself it was inadequate to explain or predict actual, concrete economic

[1] Frazer is suggested as one of Pareto's sources by his translator in a footnote to § 2142.

[2] § 1698. By 'combinations' Pareto means practices of any kind by which, rightly or wrongly, people believe they can attain a given result by a given method.

behaviour. It was this which at the end of his life impelled him to undertake his treatise on sociology. The social system, he thought, was far more complicated than the economic system.[1] Economic behaviour, so far as it *is* strictly economic, is logical, and the same may be true of certain other limited aspects of social behaviour. Such behaviour is generated by sentiments of 'interest', and interests are a special form of residue 'of such great intrinsic importance in the social equilibrium that they are best considered apart from residues'.[2] Whether considered from the point of view of the individual, or of a social group, or of society as a whole, *interests* are those states of mind which look realistically and objectively towards the maximization and efficient use of resources, themselves the means to given ends. One (but only one) of these ends, implicit in all activity, is survival, whether of individual, group or society; and, along with survival, health, strength and prosperity. An interest is a concern with material well-being, which can be assessed materially and brought within range of logico-experimental procedures. Only so much of this concern as is objectively well-based, by the best available scientific criteria, as well as being subjectively perceived as 'an interest', is to be accounted a genuine interest; the rest is a penumbra of pseudo-interest, an invasion of objectivity by misinformation and subjectivity. But this is only one of the types of concern which motivate individuals, groups and societies. It is not the interests, but the rest of the residues, which complicate the working of the social system and make it difficult to bring it within range of the scientific method.

Marx had stressed the importance of interests. Pareto's main innovation is the decisive role he attributes to the residues, and we must be as clear as possible about what they signified in his scheme of thought. We should not, for example, over-hastily identify them with 'norms', 'values', 'ultimate ends' and other mental entities invoked by other sociologists. Pareto's classification

[1] See § 2079. [2] § 1207.

of residues will help to show the sort of entities with which we have to deal. He classifies them into six classes, with many sub-classes. In any concrete case of social behaviour or socially-conditioned thought, more than one class of residue is likely to be involved. It is open to question whether the classes are strictly comparable with each other, whether they exhaust the whole range, and whether Pareto has hit on the most appropriate taxonomy. None the less, his classification was, and I think remains, an aid to clarity.

Class I is the human tendency to try out all sorts of 'combinations', methods, mixtures, devices, practices. This is the tendency which leads towards logic and experiment, but which is mainly manifested in magic and superstition and in operations which have no rational justification.

Class II is the human tendency to adhere to certain preconceived ideas, especially about social units and their embodiment in gods and similar personifications; this Pareto calls 'the persistence of aggregates'.

While Class I leads to innovation, Class II leads to conservatism. The ratio between these classes in a given society is therefore important. According to Pareto it tends to vary or oscillate.

Class III is the human need to express sentiments by external acts. Pareto is largely thinking of ritual and similar 'expressive' behaviour, but residues in this class could include all tendencies to activity rather than passivity. They are the social expression of the innate restlessness of human beings, the urge to deploy their surplus energy.

Classes IV and V comprise specifically social axioms. Residues in Class IV are those which emphasize 'sociality', or mutual obligation and reciprocity: the sociologist's residues *par excellence*. Residues in Class V concern the integrity of the individual (including freedom from pollution or sin) and of his private property. Interests belong to this Class, but there are, in addition to them, other non-economic, psychological aspects of sentiment about property and power.

Class VI consists of residues related to the sexual instinct both directly and indirectly. 'Mere sexual appetite' writes Pareto, 'is no concern of ours . . . We are interested in it only in so far as it influences theories, modes of thinking—as a residue.'[1] It is the cultural expression of displaced or repressed sexuality that Pareto here has in mind. He makes no reference to Freud.

Residues are more permanent, less shifting than derivations. Yet they are not immutable and they do shift. They stand therefore between the instinctual, biological elements which are *few and fixed*, and the rationalizing elements, which are *diverse and variable*. They are characteristically human, socio-cultural, socially transmitted, pre-logical (or proto-logical) tendencies in thought and behaviour. That Pareto thought of them as culturally rather than genetically transmitted is proved by his examples of the way in which they may vary in distribution as between different societies, occupations, social classes and historical periods. Thus he writes: 'The fact that classes of residues change but slightly or not at all in a given society over a given period of time does not mean that they may not differ very widely in different societies.'[2] He refers as examples to the differences between Sparta, Athens, Rome, England and France which he has discussed in an earlier part of his treatise.[3]

Again: 'Residues are not evenly distributed nor are they of equal intensities in the various strata of a given society. The fact is a commonplace and has been familiar in every age. The neophobia and superstition of the lower classes has often been remarked, and it is a well-known fact of history that they were the last to abandon faith in the religion which derived its very name, paganism ('ruralism'), from them. The residues of widest diffusion and greatest intensity in the uneducated are referable to Classes II and III (activity), whereas the opposite is often the case with the residues of our Class V (individual integrity).'[4]

'The minority who make up the higher classes are subject to

[1] § 1324.   [2] § 1720.   [3] § 180–1, 224–44.   [4] § 1723.

wide and sudden changes in sentiments, styles of expression, fashions and so on. It is about these exceptional groups that history and literature mainly tells us, and we are left largely in ignorance about the states of mind and customs of the mass of the population.'[1]

Pareto points out that uneducated people for the most part are not worried by contradictions between residues and between derivations. This is an important point because it follows that the spread of education will lead to an increase in the number who worry about such contradictions. Such an increase is apparent with the development of industrialization. Although Pareto stressed the non-logical motivation of much human behaviour, he also was well aware of the generalized effect of the rapid growth of scientific knowledge. On the one hand he emphasizes that in the present age of science people are not nearly so free from pre-scientific ways of thinking as they believe. Yet *some* change at the same time he allows:

'If superstition has on the whole fallen off in the masses in our day, the fact is due not so much directly to the influence of the logico-experimental sciences as indirectly to the prestige of scientists—they meantime having introduced quite a number of new superstitions of their own. And it is partly due to the enormous development of industrial life, which is to a large extent an experimental life and has had the effect of disputing— in no very explicit way, to be sure—the dominion of sentiment.'[2]

However Pareto suggests that in an industrial society there are mechanisms by which the derivation—contradictory as it often is—retains its force: 'The efficacy of a faith in spurring man to vigorous action is the greater, the simpler, the more nearly absolute, the less involved in qualification, the less ambiguous, it is, and the farther it stands removed from scientific scepticism. And from that it follows that the derivation, so far as it aims at spurring men to action, uses simple principles that over-step realities and aim at goals that lie beyond them,

[1] § 1733, 1734.   [2] § 984.

sometimes far far beyond . . . Therefore, if people acting on derivations approximate reality, it is clear that the divergence between derivations and reality must somehow or other have been corrected. The correction is obtained through the conflict and composition of the many derivations current in a society.' Pareto uses the term *composition* in the technical sense, borrowed from mechanics, in which two forces acting in two different directions are resolved into a force acting in a third direction. To take the simplest case, two directly contradictory derivations, A and B, partially cancel each other out. 'The more complex, but also the more frequent, form is the case where there are many derivations, A, B, C, . . . that are not directly contradictory, and which, when combined and mutually composed, give a resultant that approximates reality more closely than any one of them singly; and examples would be the many derivations concerning the law of nations, patriotic selfishness, the independence of the courts, reasons of state, abolition of interest on money, the advantages of increasing the public debt, and so on, which are all derivations observable among all civilized peoples.'[1]

At many points in his discussion, Pareto emphasizes that although he may ridicule the intellectual pretensions of social doctrines and expose their pseudo-logicality, he does not question that a given social doctrine may have 'social utility' under given circumstances. By 'social utility' he means utility for maintaining the cohesiveness of a society or social group, something which is neither 'good' nor 'bad' in itself, but which may, in some circumstances, be a pre-requisite for the 'practical purpose of human beings' which he defines as 'the welfare and prosperity of themselves and their societies'.[2] The formulation of goals in ideal or imaginary terms may help towards the attainment of these 'practical objectives'. He seeks to clarify his exposition by a graph:

[1] § 1772. Compare G. Myrdal, *The Political Element in Economic Theory.*
[2] § 1874.

85

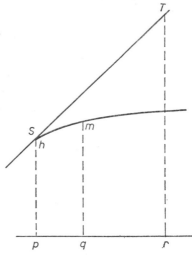

'An individual finds himself, let us say at h, where he is enjoying a certain amount of utility represented by the index ph. The idea is to induce him to go on to m, where he will enjoy a greater utility, qm. To state the matter to him in that fashion would amount to little in the way of rousing him to action. It is wiser, therefore, to put before his eyes the point T, located at quite a distance from the curve hm on the tangent hT, where he would enjoy an enormous, though altogether fantastic, utility, rT. The result now is somewhat analogous to what happens in the case where a material point is moved by a tangential force, hT, along a curve, hm. That is to say, the individual aspires to T, and moves towards T, but hampered by all sorts of practical ties (correlations, checks) he cannot hold to the tangent hT. He is forced to keep to the curve and ends up at m, whither, however, he might never have gone had he not been stimulated by a tangential impulse along the line hT.'[1] 'A being capable of non-logical conduct only could be pushed from h to m unawares. But the human being is a logical animal. He wants to know *why* he is moving in the direction hm. And so a person who is moved by instinct, interest, or other pressures along the course hm exercises his imagination and hitches his wagon to the star T. Then, through group persistences, the imaginary goal T acquires potency as sentiment in him and comes to serve, even independently of other causes, to urge him along the course hm. And it exerts the same influence upon other individuals, who find the sentiment ready-

[1] § 1869.

made in the society in which they live, and would have no other reasons, or very indifferent ones, for moving along the line *hm*.'[1] 'It is essential to distinguish the purpose, T-α, that an individual has of his own accord, from the purpose, T-β, that others may try to induce him to have. That distinction is of immense importance in human societies because of the conflict the individual feels between his own advantage and the advantage of other individuals or society. The history of morals and law is, one may say, the history of the efforts that have been made to reconcile, by fair means or foul, those two sorts of utility.'[2]

Pareto is offering us here no more than a framework of analysis. 'Questions as to the utility of ideals cannot be answered in general. One must specify which ideals one is considering, and then go on to determine their relations to other social facts.'[3] There may perhaps be some proportion between 'the pursuit of imaginary ideals' and 'the pursuit of logico-experimental aims' that is more useful to society than any other proportion, but the historical tendency has been for societies to swing from one to the other. 'Keeping to surfaces one may say that in history a period of faith will be followed by a period of scepticism, which will in turn be followed by another period of faith, this by another period of scepticism, and so on. Such descriptions are not in themselves bad; but the terms "faith" and "scepticism" may be misleading, if they are thought of as referable to any particular religion or group of religions. Looking a little deeper, one may say that society is grounded on group-persistences. These manifest themselves in residues which, from the logico-experimental standpoint, are false, and sometimes patently absurd. When, therefore, the aspect of social utility predominates to any large extent, doctrines favourable to the sentiments of group-persistence are accepted, instinctively or otherwise. When, however, the logico-experimental aspect predominates, even to some slight extent, such

[1] § 1871.   [2] § 1877.   [3] § 1882.

doctrines are rejected and replaced by others that accord in appearances, though rarely in substance, with logico-experimental science. So the human mind oscillates between the two extremes, and being unable to halt at either, continues in movement indefinitely. There might be a resting place, at least for a portion of the intellectual ruling class, if individuals here and there would consent to be persuaded that a belief may be useful to society even though experimentally false or absurd. Those few who look at social phenomena exclusively or at beliefs of others—not their own—may hold that view; and in fact we see traces of it in scientists, and we find it more or less explicit, more or less disguised, in public men who approach matters empirically. But the majority of human beings, people who are neither exclusively scientists nor far-sighted statesmen, people who do not lead but are led, and think more of their own beliefs than of the beliefs of others, can hardly hold such a view, either because of ignorance or because there is a distressing contradiction between having a faith that is to inspire vigorous action and considering that faith absurd.'[1]

Without necessarily agreeing with Pareto that human faiths are 'false' or 'absurd', we may well feel that he is justified in suggesting that most people over-estimate the evidence on which they base their deepest convictions, and that this over-estimation is in some sense necessary to them as individuals as well as to the social systems within which they are enrolled. Another phenomenon of over-estimation that is recognized and accepted as desirable among most civilized people is that which constitutes 'being in love' with another individual. The love-object is notoriously seen in a rosy light, and the lover's judgement is not arrived at logico-experimentally. Yet though recognizing its risks, social opinion is by and large on the side of this kind of over-estimation, on the grounds that it gives happiness and does more good than harm. Moreover, it is pro-

---

[1] § 2341. I quote at length, partly because *The Mind and Society* has been out of print for many years.

ductive of energy, and some of this energy can be utilized for purposes which are socially approved and conducive to the maintenance of society. The idealized purposes which are the 'stars,' in Pareto's phrase, to which are hitched human and social aspirations are also attended by possibilities of disillusionment and suffering. Perhaps we should look on these purposes, in ourselves and other people, with the same awareness, the same combination of detachment and acceptance of commitment, that we try to adopt towards the state of being in love.

'Love' is itself obviously an extremely complex idea, comprehending not only various manifestations of sexuality and eroticism, but also emotional bonds of a non-sexual or indirectly sexual kind, between friends or between members of a family or other group, between masters and their servants, subjects and their rulers, gods and their devotees. Freud, by emphasizing the element of sexuality in all these emotional bonds, was by implication stating a major hypothesis about the way, or about one way, in which a human society or group is held together. In his later writings he discusses this explicitly, expecially in *Civilization and its Discontents.* This fascinating essay does not set out to be more than a series of reflections on an aspect of the human individual which interested Freud increasingly, his sociality and rationality, seemingly at the opposite pole from those intensely self-centred irrational unconscious aspects which Freud sought to explain by the method of psycho-analysis. A comparison of this side of his thought with that of Pareto is unavoidable.

One may notice, first of all, a certain family resemblance between those somewhat shadowy entities, the residues, and such Freudian concepts as the super-ego, the Oedipus complex, narcissism and anal erotism. These concepts and the residues have this in common: they are human, they are based on man's biological nature but they are culturally developed from it within a social context. Take for example anal erotism. Only human beings make such a fuss about excrement and induce in their infants the complicated ambivalent patterns of behaviour and feeling that lead to what Freud called the ánal component in the human character, with its obsessive orderliness and parsimony, its traits of sadism and masochism and its aesthetic and plastic sublimations. Freud's concept of the anal character might well be seen as overlapping Pareto's Class V residues, those which concern property, personal integrity and pollution. Even more obviously Freudian are the Class VI residues, relating to sex. The human tendencies comprised in the other four Classes of residues are all illuminated in one way or another by Freud's ideas.

Pareto, as we have seen, deliberately refrained from hypotheses about the psychological origins of the residues. Freud, in effect, supplied hypotheses which fill this gap; hypotheses which, while no more final than Pareto's classification of the residues, are the stock in trade of modern speculation. Of particular relevance to our discussion was Freud's hypothesis that in their social behaviour people are motivated not only by rational, conscious considerations but by non-rational, largely unconscious elements originating at a primitive, infantile level of the mind. According to Freud, there can be found at this level a force which harshly forbids the animal instincts their full expression. Civilization depends on the renunciation of uninhibited sexuality and uninhibited aggressiveness. These animalities are replaced by family affection and by the more diffuse bonds of co-operation and loyalty that unite larger social groups. As civilization develops, so the social group with which the individual has an emotional bond becomes larger and more comprehensive until eventually it embraces all mankind. Freud was deeply convinced that this was leading or might lead to an excessive strain on the individual, who was being asked to renounce his animal nature to an impossible extent through the ideal demands of the universal religions, of civilized moralities and of such political doctrines as socialism and internationalism. 'Culture' he writes, 'endeavours to bind the members of the community to one another by libidinal ties . . . it makes use of every means and favours every avenue by which powerful identifications can be created among them . . . it exacts a heavy toll of aim-inhibited libido in order to strengthen communities by bonds of friendship between the members. Restrictions upon sexual life are unavoidable if this object is to be attained.'[1] At the same time the 'tendency to aggression which we can detect in ourselves and rightly presume to be present in others is the factor that disturbs our relations with our neighbours and makes it necessary for culture to institute its high demands. Civilized society is perpetually menaced with disintegration through this primary hostility of men towards one another. Their interests in their common work would not hold them together; the passions of instinct are stronger than reasoned interests. Culture has to call up every possible reinforcement in order to erect barriers against the aggressive instincts of men and hold their manifestations in check by reaction-formations in men's minds. Hence its system of methods by which mankind is to be driven to identifications and aim-inhibited love-relationships; hence the restrictions on sexual life; and hence, too, its ideal command to love one's neighbour as oneself'.[2]

Freud's criticism of present-day civilization did not necessarily imply that we ought to 'put the clock back' and return to a more primitive state. He considered, on the evidence known to him, that 'with regard to the primitive human types living at the present time, careful investigation has revealed that their instinctual life is by no means to be envied on account of its freedom'.[3] However, 'a high-water mark' in the restriction of sexuality 'has been reached in our Western European civilization'.[4] Possibly, since 1930 when the essay was published,

[1] *Civilization and its Discontents*, p. 80.

[2] *Ibid.*, p. 86. Studies of animal behaviour have shown that there are interesting mechanisms by which aggression between members of the same species can be averted by suitable behaviour.

[3] *Ibid.*, p. 92.   [4] *Ibid.*, p. 74.

Freud's own teaching has already brought some change in this respect. 'We may expect' he says 'that in the course of time changes will be carried out in our civilization so that it becomes more satisfying to our needs and no longer open to the reproaches we have made against it.'[1] The idea that the future may hold a 'Freudian revolution' in the ordering of society has been developed quite recently in two remarkable works, *Eros and Civilization*, by Herbert Marcuse, and *Life against Death*, by Norman O. Brown. But Freud himself was cautious about the possibility of a 'non-repressive civilization'. 'Perhaps' he continues 'we shall also accustom ourselves to the idea that there are certain difficulties inherent in the very nature of culture which will not yield to any efforts at reform.'

In tentative and speculative fashion, Freud suggested that there was an 'analogy between the process of cultural evolution and the path of individual development . . . It can be maintained that the community, too, develops a super-ego, under whose influence cultural evolution proceeds . . . The super-ego of any given epoch of civilization originates in the same way as that of an individual; it is based on the impression left behind them by great leading personalities, men of outstanding force of mind, or men in whom some one human tendency has developed in unusual strength and purity, often for that reason very disproportionately'.[2] 'In our investigations and our therapy of the neuroses we cannot avoid finding fault with the super-ego of the individual on two counts: in commanding and prohibiting with such severity it troubles too little about the happiness of the ego, and it fails to take into account sufficiently the difficulties in the way of obeying it—the strength of instinctual cravings in the id and the hardships of external environment. Consequently in our therapy we often find ourselves obliged to do battle with the super-ego and work to moderate its demands. Exactly the same objections can be made against the ethical standards of the cultural super-ego.

[1] *Ibid.*, p. 92.   [2] *Ibid.*, p. 137.

It, too, does not trouble enough about the mental constitution of human beings; it enjoins a command and never asks whether or not it is possible for them to obey it.'[1] The moral injunctions to which Freud refers are in fact those which originate in the second stage of social eidos, and the 'great leading personalities' who bequeathed them to the cultural super-ego were, in the first instance, the 'Great Teachers' who inaugurated that stage. Ancient teachings, long by-passed and ignored, had re-emerged in a modern context of rationality and social idealism. Freud was uneasily aware that the modern 'religion of humanity' might make demands even more excessive than those of the earlier universal religions in their pure, uncompromising forms.

Pareto and Freud alike set out to demonstrate the irrational behind the apparently rational precepts of social ethics. Pareto's main concern with them is because they make difficult, perhaps even impossible, a rational science of sociology. Freud's main concern with them is because they contribute to the excessive burden of repression—excessive in terms of its clinical effects—which the individual is called upon to bear as a member of civilized society. Pareto does not dispute the social utility of ideals; he points out that they are irrational constructions on irrational foundations. Freud makes the further point that they are irrational in their use of the irrational, that they push it to limits which endanger the health of the individual and which make the structure of the civilization itself precarious. Yet Freud does not reject the constructive work of civilization any more than does Pareto. For each of them, a rational and scientific analysis of the irrational gives ultimate hope of a kind of economics of psychic effort and satisfaction, even though both of them remain doubtful as to how far it is possible to go with it in the foreseeable future and are therefore somewhat pessimistic about the short and middle-term prospects of mankind.

[1] *Ibid.*, p. 139.

93

Chapter 4

VALUES, IDEAS AND THE SOCIAL SYSTEM[1]

M ost Anglo-Saxon readers approach the works of Durkheim and Weber at a certain disadvantage because of
unfamiliarity with their philosophical backgrounds. Where any
French or German student has at least a philosophical vocabulary, a British or American student is philosophically either
completely illiterate or else brought up, most often, in a school
of philosophy which takes rather little account of the philosophies of other countries or of other centuries. This is particularly a barrier to the penetration of German thought, diverse,
complex, partly untranslated and developing in isolation from
the rest of Europe. In the eighteen-forties, Marx and Engels
had hoped to 'discredit the philosophic struggle with the shadows
of reality, which appeals to the dreamy and muddled German
nation',[2] but the struggle has gone on unabated to this day.
In turning the pages of a German philosopher, one enters
another world and breathes another air, at times intoxicating,
at times faintly stupefying to the unhabituated. The German
style of philosophizing has indeed in this century made some
inroads among the French. The German style of sociology, with
which it is inevitably linked, has in the past quarter century

[1] Readers not concerned with Talcott Parsons' contribution to theoretical
sociology may skip this chapter without losing the general thread of the
exposition. I return to the topic of 'values' in Part III, Chapter 2.
[2] See above, p. 65.

94

made some headway in the United States and, re-exported from there, even in England. The awe with which it is received is partly due, I suspect, not so much to its intrinsic interest as to the whiff it brings with it of the 'philosophic struggle' still continuing across the Rhine.

Immanuel Kant (1724–1804), most famous of all German philosophers, set on foot the philosophic discussion of 'values' and the problem of their validity, a discussion that was popularized by the scientist and philosopher R. H. Lotze (1817–81), the theologian A. Ritschl (1822–89) and the moralistic anti-moralist Friedrich Nietzsche (1844–1900). It was developed afresh by the 'Neo-Kantians', a group who debated the distinction between the natural sciences and the social or cultural 'sciences', and whose interests were as much in history and sociology as in philosophy. Of all those who have taken part in this debate and contributed to the 'theory of value', the best known to sociologists outside Germany at the present time is undoubtedly Max Weber (1864–1920), largely owing to Parson's exposition of his ideas in *The Structure of Social Action*. Other German sociological philosophers, or philosophical sociologists, of note include W. Dilthey (1833–1911), G. Simmel (1858–1918) and M. Scheler (1874–1928), all of whom have links with Weber. So also have the philosophers E. Husserl (1859–1938), E. Cassirer (1874–1945) and K. Jaspers (1883–). There was nothing quite like the German stress on values in sociology, outside Germany, before the present century, except perhaps for A. Fouillée (1838–1912) in France, with his notion of 'idea forces', and F. H. Giddings (1855–1931) in America, who used the term 'social values'. But one of Durkheim's later writings was on 'Judgments of Reality and Judgments of Value'[1] and the terminology of value has been taken over by those sociologists and social anthropologists in France and Britain who may be considered as in some sense of

[1] In *Revue de métaphysique et de morale*, 1911. A translation is included in E. Durkheim, *Sociology and Philosophy*, 1953.

the school of Durkheim.[1] It has also increasingly come into the discussion of ethics, politics and aesthetics both among professional philosophers and at a popular level. It is in fact by 1962 part of the jargon of the day. In addition, economists have throughout the history of economics been debating the theory of *economic* value, usually as a separate issue.

In this chapter it is my aim to examine the part played by values and ideas in the theory of the social system which Parsons has largely based on his reading of Durkheim and Weber. A social system is a system of social interaction (called by Parsons, following Weber, simply 'action') between individual human actors. 'Thus conceived, a social system is only one of three aspects of the structuring of a completely concrete system of social action. The other two are the personality systems of the individual actors and the cultural system which is built into their action.'[2] The idea of a cultural system being 'built in' to a system of action is derived from Durkheim, whose concepts Parsons claims are in convergence with those of Freud. The focus of interest in our present discussion is on the nature of this 'cultural system' as described by Parsons and on the sense in which it is 'built in' to the total system of social action.

Parson's complex analysis of the constituent elements of a 'cultural system' takes its start from a three-fold classification of 'modes of orientation of action'. These three modes are the cognitive, the cathectic and the evaluative. The first of these needs no explanation. The term 'cathectic' is based on Freud's use of the word cathexis,[3] but given a wide and almost mechan-

---

[1] The use of the term 'value' by British social anthropologists is free from Kantian overtones. For example: 'When two or more persons have a *common interest* in an object, that object can be said to have a *social value* for the persons thus associated. . . . The study of social values in this sense is therefore a part of the study of social structure.' (A. R. Radcliffe-Brown, *Structure and Function in Primitive Society*, p. 199.)

[2] T. Parsons, *The Social System*, p. 6.

[3] See, for example, S. Freud, *Collected Papers*, vol. IV, p. 30. 'On Narcissism.'

ical application to mean simply 'the tendency to react positively or negatively to objects'. The evaluative mode is a synthesis of the cognitive and the cathectic modes. Parsons is of course not asserting that these modes are separable empirically; their separation and re-combination is an analytical artefact.

Parsons distinguishes in all his writings between, on the one hand, ideas or systems of belief, which are cognitive, and other mental elements which are for him in a sociological sense more fundamental and pertain to the evaluative mode. These other elements appear under slightly different guises in different places in his work. In *The Structure of Social Action* they are 'ultimate value attitudes'. In *The Social System* they are 'value-orientation patterns'. Elsewhere they are described as 'moral norms', 'role expectations' or 'evaluative standards'. These terms denote if not identical at least closely related entities, and they are all contrasted with cognitive ideas and beliefs.

'It is convenient' we read 'to distinguish the following three major classes of culture patterns. (1) Systems of ideas or beliefs. Although cathexis and evaluation are always present as orientational components, these cultural systems are characterized by a primacy of cognitive interests. (2) Systems of expressive symbols: for instance, art forms and styles. These systems are characterized by a primacy of cathectic interests. (3) Systems of value-orientations. Here the primary interest is in the evaluation of alternatives from the viewpoint of their consequences or implications for a system of action or one of its sub-systems.'[1]

May it not be redundant to distinguish between systems of belief with an evaluative component and systems of value-orientations which presumably include a cognitive component? The danger is that the redundant entities, which one cannot isolate or inspect, may be alleged as the secret springs which move the social system, without which it cannot move, and thanks to which it can only move in the particular way it does. If they were ideas or beliefs, one could check on whether people

[1] T. Parsons *et al.*, *Towards a General Theory of Action*, p. 8.

VALUES, IDEAS AND THE SOCIAL SYSTEM

had them and how far their action was connected with them. But Parsons is quite definite that they are *not* ideas or beliefs. What, then, are they?

The answer is elusive. In Parsons' earlier book *The Structure of Social Action* one is groping with him towards some consistency of which he has caught glimpses between the thought of Pareto, Durkheim and Weber and within the thought of each of them. 'A society, as Durkheim expressed it, is a "moral community" and only in so far as it is such does it possess stability . . . Durkheim arrives at the position that a common value system is one of the required conditions for a society to be a stable system in equilibrium . . . The features of this value system relevant to action cannot be exhausted by its cognitive aspect. For to understand a norm and its consequences for action is not *ipso facto* to acknowledge it as morally binding. In addition to the cognitive element there is that of the attitude of respect.'[1] In a note defining his use of the concept 'normative', the gist is that a 'normative' element in a system of action must always 'involve a sentiment . . . that something is an end in itself, regardless of its status as a means to any other end'.[2] Actions are linked together in long chains 'so arranged that what is from one point of view an end to which means are applied is from another a means to some further end' but 'logical necessity leads sooner or later to an ultimate end, that is, one which

[1] *The Structure of Social Action*, p. 389.

[2] *Ibid.*, p. 75. The psychologist W. Wundt introduced the terms 'norm' and 'normative science' in his book *Ethik* (1886) (translated by Julia Gulliver and E. B. Titchener as *Ethics: The Facts of the Moral Life*, 1897). In his *Introduction to Moral Science*, G. Simmel wrote 'A normative science does not "normalize" anything; it simply expounds or explains the norms and their interconnections'. A similar position is taken by L. Lévy-Bruhl in *La Morale et la science des moeurs*. (Translated by Elizabeth Lee as *Ethics and Moral Science*, 1905. See p. 9, *et seq.*) The American philosopher C. S. Peirce was writing about 'normative sciences' in 1903. (See his *Collected Papers*, vol. I, p. 311, *et seq.*) The terminology of 'norm' and 'normative' does not seem to have been prominent in American sociology before Talcott Parsons' use of it cited above, but since then it has become very widespread.

98

cannot be regarded as a means to any further end'. Within a given system of social action, 'the ultimate ends of different chains cannot be related to each other at random but must to a significant extent constitute a coherent system'.[1] The majority of members of 'concrete societies' are not normally conscious that there is any system of common ends, but this does not lessen the 'theoretical importance' of what Parsons calls 'the sociologistic theorem'.[2] Though individuals cannot formulate their ultimate ends or those of society precisely, their 'ultimate value attitudes' must attain a minimum level of integration for the society to *be* a society. Thus 'only in so far as the attitudes derived from the doctrines of karma and transmigration are common to all Hindus is caste legitimized and only in so far as the Protestant ethic was common to large numbers was there adequate motivation to rational ascetic mastery over everyday life'.[3] There is clearly a distinction here between full-fledged 'doctrines' and the 'attitudes' which go with such doctrines. 'It is certain that, for instance, the mass influence of the Calvinistic theology cannot be limited to those persons who have had a completely clear intellectual grasp of the theological system in Calvin's statement.'[4] Thus we arrive at the concept of the relatively vague 'ultimate value attitudes' as providing the 'common value system' of a society.

But in Parsons' subsequent writings, for example in *The Social System* (1951), these crucial attitudes are no longer described as 'ultimate'; the word is not to be found in its index. Prominent in that index, however, is the word 'role', which contrariwise is not to be found in the index of his earlier book. This change of emphasis is partly explained by the decision that 'for most purposes of the more macroscopic analysis of social systems, it is convenient to make use of a higher order unit than the act, namely the "status-role" '.[5] The terminology of 'social action' and its 'ultimate ends' comes from Max

---

[1] *Ibid.*, pp. 229–31.   [2] *Ibid.*, p. 248.   [3] *Ibid.*, p. 670.
[4] *Ibid.*, p. 605.   [5] *The Social System*, p. 25.

VALUES, IDEAS AND THE SOCIAL SYSTEM

Weber's *Theory of Social and Economic Organization*; in this work Weber does not use a term equivalent to 'role'.[1] Individuals in society play social roles and are accorded social statuses; status and role are two aspects of the way in which the position of the individual is defined in society; hence one may speak of status roles. 'The role is that organized sector of an actor's orientation which constitutes and defines his participation in an inter-active process. It involves a set of complementary expectations concerning his own actions and those of others with whom he interacts. Both the actor and those with whom he interacts possess these expectations.'[2] There can be abstracted from society, viewed as a system of inter-locking roles, a generalized 'consistency of pattern' in its role-expectations. This abstraction more or less corresponds with the 'ultimate value attitudes' of the earlier approach.

The later treatment also makes use of a modified version of Freudian psychology. Cultural patterns may be 'internalized' to become part of the structure of the individual personality. 'Particular importance is to be attributed to the internalization of value-orientations, some of which become part of the super-ego structure of the personality and, with corresponding frequency, of institutionalized role-expectations.'[3] Freud followed Ferenczi in using the term 'internalization' (or 'introjection') to describe a mental process by which children imagine themselves to have incorporated within themselves their parents and various sorts of 'good' and 'bad' objects. Although in this vivid, concrete sense the feeling of having incorporated these objects remains at an unconscious level, the process is important for

---

[1] As Nadel pointed out (in *The Theory of Social Structure*, p. 22) the first explicit formulation of the concept of role is in the American philosopher George Mead's *Mind, Self and Society* (1934) and the American anthropologist Ralph Linton's *The Study of Man* (1936), since when the usage has become general. The analysis of the relationship between 'self' and 'society' has a strong tradition in American sociology, from Cooley's *Human Nature and the Social Order* (1902) to Riesman's *Lonely Crowd* (1950).

[2] *Towards a General Theory of Action*, p. 23.   [3] *Ibid.*, p. 22.

the formation and development of the super-ego, since it is the basis of the adult's feeling that there is an inner voice which tells him to do something or, more often, that he must not do something. The importance of this inner voice in the working of society is obvious, and Freud did in fact look on this internalized self-within-the-self as the origin of all morality. He also regarded it as, in one of its aspects, a severe and primitive taskmaster. He distinguished between the crude coercion on the ego exercised by the super-ego and the constraint of outside circumstances on the ego, which it consciously recognizes and accepts as limiting the fulfilment of its aims in the light of what Freud called 'the reality principle.'

But Parsons uses the term 'internalization' much more widely to include the whole process of assimilation by the individual from infancy onwards of the cultural elements in his environment. Everything he learns about himself and his environment is learnt socially and therefore the whole process of learning is in fact a process of absorbing from the social group with whom he comes in contact a selection of their knowledge, beliefs, ideas, standards and so on. In his essay on 'The Super-ego and the Theory of Social Systems', Parsons makes quite explicit the difference between his viewpoint and that of Freud, who, he says, 'introduced an unreal separation between the super-ego and the ego . . . The distinction which Freud makes between the super-ego and the ego—that the former is internalized, by identification, and that the latter seems to consist of responses to external reality rather than of internalized culture—is not tenable'.[1] 'Freud's insight was profoundly correct when he focussed on the element of moral standards. This is, indeed, central and crucial, but it does seem that Freud's view was too narrow. The inescapable conclusion is that not only moral standards, but *all the components of the common culture* are internalized as part of the personality structure.'[2] Whereas to Freud the moral standards are linked with the super-ego and tend to

[1] *Working Papers in the Theory of Action*, p. 19.   [2] *Ibid.*, p.18.

be unrealistic, to Parsons the whole development of the ego is seen in moral terms, since morality is intrinsic to social inter-action and all cultural learning is social and therefore moral. This of course represents Durkheim's major contribution to Parsons' theory. From Parsons' point of view, Freud 'failed to take explicitly into account the fact that the frame of reference in terms of which objects are cognized, and therefore adapted to, is cultural and thus cannot be taken for granted as given, but must be internalized as a condition of the development of mature ego-functioning'.[1] Thus Freud needs to be supple-mented and amended by Durkheim, while similarly 'in Durk-heim's work there are only suggestions relative to the psycho-logical mechanisms of internalization and the place of internal-ized moral values in the structure of personality itself'.[2] It is only when, as in Parsons' own theory, the ideas of Durkheim and Freud are combined and adjusted, that the sociological and psychological interpretations of social behaviour can in his view be fully integrated. I would myself prefer to see Freud, without so drastic a modification, combined with Pareto rather than Durkheim.

To recapitulate, Parsons' four main approaches to the defini-tion of the crucial 'systems of value-orientations' may be sum-marized as (1) starting from Durkheim's concept of a common value system as one of the required conditions for a society to be a stable system in equilibrium; (2) starting from Weber's con-cept of ultimate ends, and the argument that every chain of actions must point towards such ends; (3) starting from the concept of social roles, and arguing that in any society there must be a generalized consistency of pattern in its role-expecta-tions; (4) starting from Freud's concept of the internalized super-ego, and arguing that the common value system is both internalized in the individual personality and externally existent as a shared system of symbols.

Although Parsons gives evaluation prior importance in the

[1] *Ibid.*, p. 19.   [2] *Ibid.*, p. 15.

social system, he by no means denies the importance of cognition.[1] 'The primary emphasis of this volume' he writes in *The Social System* 'has been on the integration of social systems at the level of patterns of value-orientation as institutionalized in role-expectations. These patterns of value-orientation are elements of the cultural tradition, but are only part of it. Man is a cognizing animal, and so his values do not exist apart from beliefs which give them cognitive meaning . . . Furthermore, of course, the general strain to consistency in a cultural tradition, the more so the more highly "rationalized" it is, means that in general the value-orientations tend to be relatively consistent with the belief system . . . If ideological beliefs and value-patterns are, as assumed, interdependent, relative stability and consistency of the belief system has the same order of functional significance as do stability and consistency of the value-orientation patterns. Hence there must be a set of beliefs, subscription to which is in some sense an obligation of collectivity membership roles, where the cognitive conviction of truth and the "moral" conviction of rightness are merged . . . This integration may well be and generally is . . . imperfect. An approximation to it is, however, of high significance to a social system. Ideology thus serves as one of the primary bases of the cognitive legitimation of patterns of value-orientation.'[2]

This line of argument, and expecially Parsons' statement that 'values do not exist apart from beliefs' makes one wonder again how he can feel himself justified in assuming that two *separate* systems, one 'evaluative' and the other 'cognitive', exist side by side. One or the other of them is surely redundant. It may well be a peculiarity of social beliefs, at any rate in our own time, that they are to a high degree associated not only with a 'cognitive conviction of truth' but also with a 'moral conviction

[1] The 'Note on the Role of Ideas' in *The Structure of Social Action* is somewhat inconclusive. Much more to the point is Chapter 8 of *The Social System*: 'Belief Systems and the Social System: the Problem of the "Role of Ideas".' See also *Essays in Sociological Theory*: 'The Role of Ideas in Social Action.'   [2] *The Social System*, p. 350.

of rightness'. The importance of ideology, and of religion in its ideological aspect, lies in its legitimation not of 'patterns of value-orientation' but of social relationships, of the social structure itself. They explain, or appear to explain, and thereby validate the existing structure of relationships and thus to put an ideal gloss on the sociological reality. For the benefit of individuals for whom explanation, interpretation, validation are vital needs, ideologies are elaborated. For other individuals, the mere fact of being in the midst of a web of relationships is enough, most of the time, to keep them moving along the socially sanctioned path, and for them only the vaguest notions of legitimacy and validity will suffice. As we saw, Parsons himself wrote in *The Structure of Social Action* that the majority of people are not normally conscious that there is any system of common ends. The increasing education, literacy, and access-ibility to mass-communication of the majority in all major societies has indeed for some time been leading to an increase in the pervasiveness of ideologies, and in the importance of ideological debate. As Pareto realized, the sense of social pur-pose can be sustained by debate as well as by agreement, and this makes it easier to understand the internal inconsistencies and non-logicalities of the more widely diffused 'systems' (if that is the right sort of word—may be one should call them idioms or vocabularies) of social belief. In the industrial societies of the modern world one can observe a continuous and indecisive clash between rationalizations of underlying and more primitive patterns of behaviour and structures of relationship. In so far as such societies each have a 'common value system' (and in-contestably they do have *something* of that order) it is at least as much a framework of thought within which disagreement can take place as it is a basis of general consensus.

Ideologies then constitute a 'symbolic battle ground' for 'elements of tension and conflict' within the social system, and they tend to polarize. This 'process of ideological polarization' is subject to 'mechanisms of social control', of which one 'in the modern type of society' is 'through the linking of ideologies with the institutionalized pursuit of the intellectual disciplines dealing with their subject matter'.[1] Ideological debates on such questions as the merits of private enterprise and central planning, or of different forms of government, are referred to academic economists and political scientists. (This should—and does to some extent—lead to a more searching examination of underlying problems; but it also leads to a 'scholastic' or 'academic' hypertrophy of terminology and theory, in which the basic problems become, for the ordinary man, obscured and conflicts muffled.)

However the existence of institutionalized 'social sciences' with at least some degree of autonomy within the social system is clearly of high significance for the future of ideology. Parsons concludes his discussion on this point as follows: 'In this perspective it becomes clear that the social sciences have a particularly crucial, and in certain respects precarious position relative to the ideological balance of the social system. On the one hand the more important social ideologies cannot avoid concern with the subject matter of the social sciences, nor can the latter simply avoid problems which touch on ideological interests. But on the other hand, the circumstances in which ideologies are developed and operate are such, that it seems practically impossible to avoid the presence of an important area of conflict between the two major types of cognitive interest (i.e. ideological and sociological). The cognitive distortions which are always present in ideologies, often compulsively motivated, will tend to be uncovered and challenged by the social scientist. Some of the results may be accepted, but only painfully and with allowance for a process of assimilation and adjustment over time. Because of this situation there will, more or less inevitably, be a tendency for the guardians of ideological purity in a social system to be highly suspicious of what social scientists are doing.

[1] *Ibid.*, p. 358.

VALUES, IDEAS AND THE SOCIAL SYSTEM

'Indeed it is not surprising that the two non-rational mechanisms of stabilization of ideological orientations, traditionalization and authoritarian enforcement of an "official" creed, are so very commonly encountered in this field. The "liberal" pattern of freedom of thought, which both permits ideological controversy and free interplay between the scientific and the ideological levels is the exception, and certainly depends for its stability on a rather delicately balanced combination of conditions in the social system. It may, however, also be a highly important condition of many elements of the potentiality of growth of societies, as it is obviously a pre-requisite for the flourishing of social science.'[1]

It is interesting to compare this position with that of Karl Mannheim. In discussing the 'prospects of scientific politics', Mannheim suggested that a group broadly described as the intelligentsia would have the function of elaborating a social viewpoint relatively free from the special interests of different social strata. Parsons distinguishes within this group between social scientists on the one hand and, on the other, professional or institutionalized ideologists, for example the theoreticians of political parties or economic organizations. This distinction is useful. But we have to remember that in practice the social scientists are themselves often bound to stray far over onto the ideological side of the field and to purvey ideologies not only unconsciously but even deliberately. Because of the great contribution which the social sciences can make to the legitimation of a dominant ideology, there is an inevitable pressure on social scientists to shape their work and findings towards the validation of that ideology. For this reason the social sciences tend to be much more ethnocentric, much more nationally based, than the natural sciences.

[1] *Ibid.*, p. 358.

PART III
A Further Stage in Social Eidos

Chapter 1

THE SOCIAL STRUCTURE OF
SOCIAL EIDOS

In Part I and Part II I have discussed some elements in contemporary social eidos and their origins. The quest for a way of thinking about society more firmly grounded in knowledge is a continuing one. In part III I attempt to set out, without dogmatism, a framework for this continuing quest.

In the first five sections, I am concerned primarily with the sociological implications of the differential interest in ideas, and receptivity to ideas, shown by different members of society. I sketch out a model for a 'social structure of social eidos' which takes this differentiation into account. I relate this to the Marxist theory of 'ruling' ideas produced by that part of the 'ruling' class which specializes in ideas. I am led to distinguish between five ways in which individuals may be oriented towards ideas, these orientations being in part the result of the historical and social situation of the individuals concerned.

Historically, the 'believing' orientation towards ideas, and the moral and social beliefs that go with it, are seen as originating with the second stage of social eidos. In the same way, the terminology of 'value' is seen as originating with the third stage of social eidos, and as representing an attempt to reconcile the new scientific rationality with the cultural heritage of religion and morality. In ethics, Kant, and in sociology, Comte, are mainly responsible for this persistent element of moralistic rationalism, evident in Durkheim and Parsons, no less than in Hobhouse and Ginsberg.

Against it on the whole may be set the influence of Marx and Freud, and certainly of Pareto.

In the last three sections, which are necessarily the most personal, the most tentative and the most incomplete, I explore some alternative possibilities of rational development within social eidos. I suggest the notion of a socially tolerated 'unsocial eidos', articulated largely in terms of literature and the arts. I cite Bachelard's idea of society as a life-long 'school' based on the ultimate value of 'pure' science. I emphasize however the priority in the contemporary world of the 'rationality of survival' and the cultivation of a scientific technology.

Social eidos depends on the objective existence of structures of social relationship and on the perception of these structures by individuals. It is complicated not only by the over-estimation[1] that tends to go with membership but by a differentiation among the members in the type and intensiity of their social perceptions. Social eidos is not spread evenly among the members.

Social structure differentiates the access of individuals to various resources and privileges. In its different facets the structure controls access to property, to sexual rights, to authority, to knowledge, and so on. The structure of access to each special

[1] The basic idea that goes with membership of a society or social group is that membership is worthwhile, that one would rather be a member than not. In its particular form, the idea is applied to a particular society but it includes, obscurely, a sense of the advantage in membership of societies and groups in general and of the disadvantages and dangers of isolation. Particular memberships are often due to the accidents of birth, locality and so forth. But before one has learned to reflect that one's membership is involuntary, strong feelings of attachment to one's own society or group have probably grown up. As soon as one starts to think about it at all, in all likelihood, it is to one's own society and not to any other that one feels it is not only good to belong, but best to belong. At the same time, if one has any intercourse with members of other societies, one learns to allow for their feeling as strong a preference for their societies as one does for one's own. And from the outsider's point of view, one over-estimates the advantages in one's own particular membership. Put in another way, the social eidos of an average member of society is biased in its favour. Or, as Pareto would say, 'society is grounded on group-persistences'. See above, p. 87.

resource or privilege is closely related to the general social structure, but can be distinguished from it. The internal differentiations between members in general knowledge and belief thus constitute a specific sub-structure; likewise the internal differentiations in social knowledge and belief. The structure of differences in social knowledge and belief is itself perceived by the members with carrying degrees of clarity. Those who have special concern with social knowledge and belief often have theories about the desirability or otherwise of existing patterns of differentiation in this respect. To some extent therefore a pattern of differentiation in social eidos between individuals within a society is deliberately cultivated by groups which have special means of controlling it, for example by systems of initiation or education. In many societies, however, the differentiation is only partially deliberate: it also stems from factors in the environment and personality which are only imperfectly realized or controlled. The structure of a society in relation to its social eidos is therefore a complex derivative of its structure in the more general sense, and also of deliberate policy on the part of key groups, and finally also of residual factors, such as unplanned variability in the endowment of individuals and in their environments.

To recapitulate the main items in this terminology, we have (i) *general eidos*, the predominant structure and character of the whole stock of ideas available in a society or group (ii) *social eidos*, that part of the eidos which relates to social institutions and activities (iii) *general social structure*, the relatively fixed scheme of relationships in a society or group (iv) *the social structure of general eidos*, the social structure of access by individuals to the general stock of ideas and finally (v) *the social structure of social eidos*, the social structure of access by individuals to the stock of social ideas. 'Ideas' can be provisionally regarded as elements in a repertoire or vocabulary of knowledge and belief, without prejudice to the question of the status of 'values', which will come up in chapter 6.

THE SOCIAL STRUCTURE OF SOCIAL EIDOS

The five elements listed above may be viewed as five variables to be found in any society or group. Using this terminology, we can ask to what extent the variables depend upon one another. For example, we know that each different social structure has a different social eidos, so we can go on to ask the question whether different *types* of social structure go with different *types* of social eidos. This question involves trying out typologies of social structure and typologies of social eidos. In fact, using typologies of all five variables, we could ask ten formally separate questions about their interdependence, all of them aspects of the problem of how change comes about in a social structure.

Chapter 2

'RULING IDEAS' AND THE ROLE
OF THE INTELLECTUALS

In a previous chapter, we saw that Marx and Engels laid stress on the way in which 'the ideas of the ruling class are in every epoch the ruling ideas' and that these are 'nothing more than the ideal expression of the dominant material relationships'. This is in full accord with the Marxist orthodox belief in the pre-eminence of material conditions as causes of historical change. But we saw that they went on to distinguish between the 'thinkers' of the ruling class and the active members of this class who 'have less time to make up ideas and illusions about themselves'. If this distinction is empirically valid, it has important consequences for the social structure of social eidos, since the division of society into rulers and ruled, which is an expression of material interests, is paralleled by a further division between thinkers and non-thinkers, which is an expression of psychological or temperamental differences.

In recognizing that only a minority of the working class were 'class-conscious', Marx made a similar distinction between members of that class. He also pointed to the contrast in outlook between the different national bourgeoisies, especially between the German bourgeoisie from which he himself came and the English and French bourgeoisies whom in many ways he admired. He thus recognized the existence, and even the importance, of cultural and psychological as well as material differences in the endowment of individuals, groups and societies.

H   113

There is however a certain asymmetry in the Marxist analysis. In the ruling class, thinkers are contrasted with activists; but in the working class, thinking or 'consciousness' goes *with* activism; in the ruling class, thought is seen as having an inhibiting effect on activity, while in the working class, a tendency to activity on behalf of *working-class* interests impels the working-class activist into the role of thinker, while his thinking, unlike that of the ruling-class thinker, spurs him on to greater activity. The working-class activist-thinker is in fact preparing himself to take over power from his rulers. The separation between thinking and acting is a source of weakness in the ruling class; their combination in the leadership of the working class is a source of strength.

When Marx and Engels describe the ruling class as having 'control over the means of mental production', as well as over the means of material production, they are stating concisely a view of the social structure of general and social eidos which might be elaborated as follows. The means of mental production include literacy and access to books and other sources of knowledge. At the time that Marx and Engels were writing, these means were in general only available to a minority in the population. The male children of the ruling class were especially privileged in this respect, and care was taken not to extend the privilege in such a way as to undermine the *status quo*. Control over schools and universities was an important aspect of their over-all control. If however the ruling class was enterprising in seeking to extend its wealth and power, it needed to increase the proportion of literate and trained people in the population and thus to alter its social structure of general eidos in some measure. But changes in the social structure of general eidos had implications for the social structure of social eidos. The ruling class had to safeguard its position by compensating the increase in education by an increase in indoctrination. From the infant school to the university, the two processes were combined. The legitimation of their authority, to use a Weber-

114

ian phrase, had in the past been largely through the beliefs and teaching of the prevailing religious orthodoxy, and so, to a large extent, it remained, but added to this there was now a stronger admixture of national and patriotic sentiment, and also a stronger element of ideology, in the sense of political and economic pseudo-theory. The main strength of ruling class control in the sphere of mental production was twofold: firstly, they controlled the access of the young to knowledge, in a general sense, at all stages; secondly, they could insure that general eidos was imparted with a suitable addition of social eidos. Education is a long process which begins in childhood, a propitious time for the implanting of false consciousness at so deep a level that even the critical capacity of the fully adult, fully educated mind fails to recognize the distortion. The content of the social eidos had to be adapted to changing circumstances, not so as to bring it more in line with the objective situation, but so as to prevent questioning of the rightness and fitness of the existing general social structure.

Marx and Engels imply also, in their comments on the recent evolution of social eidos, that the rise of the bourgeoisie to political dominance had started something like a landslide in the realm of ideas. Old fixities had gone, and this, too, was a factor which would favour the supersession of the bourgeoisie, in its turn, by the proletariat, with relative speed. We need look no further than the Communist Manifesto for a statement on these lines: 'The bourgeoisie cannot exist without constantly revolutionizing the instruments of production, and with them the whole relations of society . . . Constant revolutionizing of production, uninterrupted disturbance of all social conditions, everlasting uncertainty and agitation distinguish the bourgeois epoch from all earlier ones. All fixed, fast frozen relations, with their train of ancient and venerable prejudices and opinions, are swept away, all new-formed ones become antiquated before they can ossify. All that is solid melts into air, all that is holy is profaned, and man is at last compelled to face with sober senses his real conditions of life and his relations with his kind.' The efforts of the ruling class through its ideologists, to provide a generally acceptable social eidos are therefore in this perspective seen as unavailing. 'Finally, in times when the class struggle nears the decisive hour, the process of dissolution going on within the ruling class, in fact within the whole range of old society, assumes such a violent, glaring character that a small section of the ruling class cuts itself adrift and joins the revolutionary class, the class that holds the future in its hands. Just as, therefore, at an earlier period, a section of the nobility went over to the bourgeoisie, so now a portion of the bourgeoisie goes over to the proletariat, and in particular a portion of the bourgeois ideologists, who have raised themselves to the level of comprehending theoretically the historical movement as a whole.'

According to the Marxist view of the social structure of general eidos and social eidos, this 'going over' of 'a portion of the bourgeois ideologists', (exemplified in Marx and Engels themselves) is of crucial importance since they have access, which the proletariat does not, to the 'means of mental production'. They provide theories for a new social eidos more objectively in accord than the old with the interests of the proletariat. This is the 'valiant aid' which Pareto[1] saw as the contribution of the intellectuals to the genuine improvement in the condition of the working-class during the nineteenth century.

Comte, Marx and Pareto, Karl Mannheim and Talcott Parsons have pointed to the significance of the social structure of social eidos in processes of social change. Perhaps the analysis would be carried a little further if we could set out the whole range of factors which differentiate the various members of society in relation to social eidos. Besides their different positions in the general social structure there are differences in their intellectual endowment and its development, differences in the amount and type of education they have received, differences in their disposition towards activism and towards intense belief,

[1] See p. 75.

THE ROLE OF THE INTELLECTUALS

differences in their type of cultural interest, e.g. religious, artistic, scientific, etc. This list is illustrative rather than exhaustive, and intended simply to make explicit a complexity which is already implicit in the writings of, for example, Marx and Mannheim.

'Hitherto' writes Mannheim 'all classes have included, in addition to those who actually represented their direct interests, a stratum more oriented towards what might be called the realm of the spirit. Sociologically, they could be called "intellectuals" . . . We are not referring here to those who bear the outward insignia of education, but to those few among them who, consciously or unconsciously, are interested in something else than success in the competitive scheme.' Such people, Mannheim says, have always existed but the historical difference is that they are now no longer identified with a particular group struggling for its rights within society; and they will, as time goes on 'be even more than now in increasing proportions recruited from all social strata rather than merely from the most privileged ones'.[1] To plot these 'socially unattached intellectuals' on the map of the social structure of social eidos, the primary differential to look for would be educational, and next most important would be personality differences which confer on them a certain 'spirituality' and free them from the crude sway of 'interests'. Education has a major role in this, but education by itself is not enough. The scholar temperament, the willingness to be an onlooker, the unworldliness which descends from the traditions of other worldliness—these elements lurk behind the Mannheimian concept. One senses here a strong conviction about the part which Universities can play in a modern society and the part which sociology can play in the Universities. Like the 'portion of the bourgeois ideologists' who in the Communist Manifesto go over to the proletariat, the 'socially unattached intellectuals' of Mannheim are those 'who have raised themselves to the level of comprehending

[1] *Ideology and Utopia*, p. 232.

117

theoretically the historical movement as a whole'. In one sense, the general social structure is irrelevant to the pin-pointing of these individuals, since their origins may be in any part of it.[1]

Parsons, as I see it, has taken Mannheim's scheme and added to it a refinement of some importance, in distinguishing between 'the scientific and the ideological levels' of social eidos. In practice, of course, these levels, and the individuals who represent them in the intellectual division of labour, tend considerably to overlap. The most scientific social scientists and scholars may consciously or unconsciously contribute to social eidos at the ideological level; the most propagandist hacks may consciously or unconsciously be agents for the diffusion of 'scientific' social eidos. Both sorts of people specialize in social ideas, and therefore have special significance in the social structure of social eidos.

[1] But is it *so* irrelevant? The individuals concerned can, I suspect, be found clustering in certain institutions, above all in the Universities, where they have a more or less recognized style of life and, in many countries, a standard salary scale. Mannheim himself calls them a 'distinct social and intellectual *middle* stratum'. In the general social structure defined by income, or by standards of consumption, they have a middle place. In the social structure of general eidos, viewed as a hierarchy, their position is reasonably secure, though lacking the traditional prestige of high literary learning on the one hand, and the obvious achievement of natural science on the other. It is in the social structure of social eidos, by definition, that so far from being in the middle they are securely at the apex, and slowly but surely establishing a position there in every modern society, and even under communism.

Chapter 3

DISPERSED MINORITIES OF
THINKERS AND BELIEVERS

I will now attempt a rather more detailed account of the social structure of social eidos in a contemporary national society. The fact that social ideas are presented to people, and if fully accepted by them become social beliefs, is a product of two forces coming as it were from opposite directions. At one end, we have the need in the members of the society for such ideas; the willingness, and in some cases the eagerness, of individuals to 'believe', that is, to commit themselves to a definite belief. At the other end, we have the disposition of societies and other social organizations, working through individuals as agents, to propagate ideas intended to validate their existence, structure and activities. Ideas funnel out from a small number of sources to a large number of people. If one is thinking only of sources of 'original' ideas, these are very few indeed. The actual propagators of ideas, those who adapt and transmit the 'original' ideas, are more numerous but are still a small minority compared to the numbers of potential recipients. At the receiving end, however, individuals are markedly differentiated in their receptivity. A relatively small number of dispersed receptive individuals constitute a most important feature of the social structure of social eidos.

At one end we have the fountain-heads from which social ideas are flowing. At the other end we have a population of individuals differentiated both as to the amount of attention they give to ideas and as to the type of idea which they are psychologically predisposed to attend to. The attitudes of 'reason' and of 'faith' enter in some measure into all the individuals concerned, both at the transmitting and at the receiving end of the social structure of social eidos. Even in an 'age of faith' it is probable that those nearer the sources of ideas, those at the centre of the system, would incline towards more reason and less faith. In an 'age of reason' like our own, this effect is likely to be more marked still.[1]

Those concerned with ideas at the transmitting end will, broadly speaking and with exceptions, be more detached, more sophisticated, more relativistic in their attitudes than those receptive to ideas at the receiving end. This does not rule out 'faith' at the transmitting end, or 'reason' at the receiving end, but it makes it likely that the proportions of the two attitudes will vary between the two ends. The distribution of educational opportunity and attainment will emphasize this tendency. As I have already suggested, one cannot map the social structure of social eidos even approximately without taking into account a number of separate factors which differentiate individual members of a society in relation to ideas, and these factors will be at work at *both* ends of the structure.

Remembering that only a minority of the individuals at the

[1] There are however some historical factors which offset it. We are considering the social structure of social eidos in a national society and a nation is an entity which tends to elicit attitudes of faith rather than reason. Ideas about the national interest, ideas relating to national self-justification and self-criticism, mainly originate from individuals at the centre of the political system, a system in which the rhetoric of persuasion, emotive exaggeration and the cult of personality are taken for granted. The development of the mass politics of nationalism and of social reform, though relatively recent, has been based, to a large extent, on that important dispersed minority at the receiving end of the flow of ideas for whom it is a psychological need to believe strongly.

Moreover, along with politics at the centre there is still the much older non-rational fountain-head of religion. In many societies, 'old' religious ideas and 'new' political ideas flow together in a single stream. And although the universal religions are doctrinally supra-national, they have national organizations and traditions.

receiving end are at all frequently reactive to ideas of any sort, and remembering also that among this minority ideas will be more readily received if they involve a strong element of 'faith' there still remains a significant demand for ideas that are based, or appear based, on 'reason'. To what quarter can members of a society look, should they wish, for ideas of this kind in the field of social eidos? Where are they most likely to find unprejudiced opinions and interpretations? Should they turn to Mannheim's 'socially unattached intellectuals', to those individuals who are 'genuinely oriented towards what might be called the realm of the spirit', rather than towards the 'direct interests' of a nation, a class, a political party, a profession, and so on? Supposing it is the ideas of people like these that they wish to know about, how are they to get in touch with them, and how are they to identify them? They will be people whose motivation for concern with social eidos appears to be, as far as humanly possible, free of self-interest, independent of group-interest. They will also have access to information and the capacity to use 'logical' procedures, to make rational-technical use of the tools of the intellect. Those who cannot or do not use these tools are, at our stage of social eidos, open to suspicion. A double qualification, then, is required: on the one hand, purity of motive, on the other hand, trained intelligence. These qualifications point in the direction of the Universities.

Chapter 4

THE TRANSMISSION OF IDEAS AND SOCIAL IDEALS

I want now to indicate some features of the social structure of social eidos which lie between the transmitting and receiving ends and which are specialized for tasks of diffusion. The presentation of original (or relatively original) ideas makes up only a fraction of all intellectual activity. Most of it is concerned with transmission, more or less unaltered, and popularization, in simplified and sometimes vulgarized form. Much of this takes place through the processes of formal education, much of it by way of informal education in the home, the workplace, the peer-group and so on, much of it through books, newspapers and the mass media of communication. Individuals who serve as conscious agents in these processes do so from a wide range of motives, which may include the pure wish to teach, the wish for financial reward, the wish for influence and reputation and, in some cases, the wish to exploit and manipulate by means of ideas. Those who cater for mass needs in the field of ideas are by necessity less highly educated in the main, less intellectual and more in tune with non-rational popular trends, than the élite groups of mental production. After it has been through the mill of popularization, an idea will have shed most of its complexity and, perhaps, of its rationality. The knowledge of this presents a challenge to any original thinker who wishes a wide circulation for his ideas.

By undertaking the compulsory education of all the children born into them, societies provide themselves with a large 'captive' group for the reception of ideas. In doing so they pose themselves the question of what parts of social eidos should be transmitted through the schools. In some societies and in some schools, religious or political indoctrination is given an important place. In others, the major part of this function is on a separate, voluntary or quasi-voluntary basis, for example through Sunday Schools and youth organizations. But even then, some formal provision will be made in the syllabus for religious and political instruction—the latter in the form of 'civics' or 'current affairs'—and elements of social eidos will be embodied in the teaching of other subjects, notably history. The idea of education as a beneficent and creative activity, and of the moral significance of the teacher's vocation, is indeed itself everywhere a component of modern social eidos. Public policy everywhere aims at giving children more and more education, on idealistic as well as rational-technical grounds. The idealism glosses over the extent to which education is a means by which society imposes its tasks on reluctant or indifferent young people.

This resistance to school is not itself sufficiently coherent to take the form of an anti-idea among the school-children. It must however contribute to the anti-intellectualism of adults. There are similar negative, unorganized resistances to the enmeshing ideas of religion and politics. The class of those who are 'not interested' in organized religion, or 'not interested' in party politics, is not a conscious class, but it does consist of people whom religious and political organizations have tried, but failed, to interest. In order to maintain themselves, these organizations must try to hold their existing members, and win new ones. If, as in some societies, everyone is nominally enrolled in a dominant religious or political organization, then the effort goes into recruiting people who will voluntarily do more than the indispensible minimum. Social organizations, and the national society itself have to keep up a constant pressure on their members to fulfil and if possible exceed their obligations.

The social structure of social eidos is to a great extent the structure of this pressure. Virtually all individuals have a social impulse, but it varies in strength, and in the average individual it is counteracted by resistances.

In general the resistances are unorganized and inarticulate. To organize and make articulate resistance to a social pressure is to set up a social counter-pressure, for instance a League of Militant Atheists or a political party with the specific programme of ending all other political parties. The idea of contracting out does not lend itself to organization. The resistance it implies is basically a resistance against being organized. The social structure of social eidos is therefore a structure within which organized, articulate pressures are meeting not only organized, articulate counter-pressures but also unorganized, inarticulate resistances.

Historically and empirically we can see that the social impulses in individuals have been strong enough to keep societies going. But we can also see that special devices have been needed to mobilize extra effort. The success of these devices has depended on another empirical fact that we have already noted, namely the manifestation by certain individuals of exceptionally strong social impulses. By 'social impulse' we mean the willingness to subordinate oneself to the purposes of some group, and the range of such purposes is obviously very wide. But I think it would be possible to confirm empirically that those individuals who are prepared to make an exceptional effort for a group purpose are often, perhaps always, motivated not only by an exceptional interest in the purpose of the group but also by an exceptional wish, or need, to have the esteem of a group of some kind, combined with inner self-esteem.[1]

[1] But how far is this extra social impulse an inherent and constant characteristic of the individuals concerned, how far is it elicited from them by particular social configurations and circumstances? Quite possibly some individuals are born potentially more social than others, while other individuals, of average or normal innate sociality, manifest exceptional social impulses as a result of a special kind of relationship developing within a particular group.

Pareto stressed the essential distinction between 'the purpose that an individual has of his own accord' and 'the purpose that others may try to induce him to have'. The history of morals and law, he said, was the history of the efforts that have been made to reconcile the two, 'by fair means or foul'. The 'foul' means are of course the various forms of compulsion, the 'fair' are those of persuasion. Pareto assumes that among animals social behaviour is instinctive, but that human beings require a motive for it in their thought. The individual member of human society must often be reconciled to the roles he is called on to play in it, roles that involve, for example, subordination, the performance of unpleasant or fatiguing tasks, the running of physical dangers, the acceptance of burdensome responsibilities, the renunciation of sexual freedom. To some extent the individual does this under compulsion; to some extent he is induced to do so by rewards; but to an important extent also his co-operation is voluntary, and this is only possible because of the way he perceives himself in relation to his social universe.

Acceptance of membership of the group is suffcient motive for co-operation with its routine demands, but more is needed in the case of special demands. For tasks which place a strain on individual resolve, special discipline is needed, a discipline moreover which is not merely applied from outside but which the individual co-operates in applying to himself. For individuals submitting to such disciplines, social eidos in the form of strong belief is of peculiar importance. It enables them to perceive the sacrifice and suffering involved in the discipline as worth while, and this suffering heightens the emotional significance of the beliefs associated with it. A comparative sociology of the special group disciplines might deal, for instance, with initiation ceremonies, rules of apprenticeship and scholastic examinations. But the disciplines which are of particular significance here are those which are more explicitly altruistic, which stress the willingness of the individual to make a total sacrifice of his own interests, even of life itself, with rewards

125

remote and uncertain or with no reward at all. These may be characterized as disciplines of total dedication; examples may be found in the military and in the monastic sphere, or in the discipline of extremist political parties. Not all warriors, priests or partisans are involved in such disciplines, which are indeed exceptional, but they constitute an ideal of which the more average individual is aware. At certain periods and in certain situations, there are groups which approximate to the ideal discipline, and their behaviour, or that of their ideal representatives, is recorded and extolled in the annals of the cultural super-ego.

Chapter 5

FIVE ORIENTATIONS TOWARDS
IDEAS

In our scheme of the social structure of social eidos it may
help if we distinguish five main types of orientation (to use a
favourite word of Weber and Parsons) which individuals may
have towards ideas: (1) negative (2) opportunistic (3) thinking
(4) believing (5) calculating. It is assumed that the majority of
individuals have an orientation towards ideas which is of low
intensity; in extreme cases, almost completely negative, but
more commonly 'opportunistic' in the sense that in situations
where an idea is needed, the individual will take whatever is
offered, but on another occasion will take another idea without awareness of inconsistency. The more positive orientations,
'thinking', 'believing' and 'calculating', are found in a minority
only. Thinkers are interested in the process of thought rather
than the act of belief; cogitation and contemplation give them
satisfaction rather than action or identification with a group.
Believers get their satisfaction from precisely the commitment that
thinkers avoid; it is important to them that the idea they prize
should be shared with others. Both thinkers and believers put
their self-interest second to their interest in eidos, the believer
to eidos in a particular form, the thinker to eidos in general.
The calculating individual is one who is interested in eidos only
as a means to self-interested ends, and for whom the social
structure of social eidos is an exploitative structure through
which people are manipulated. Each of the three positive
orientations is self-conscious. The thinker is conscious not only

of himself as a thinker but of thinkers as a social category. By putting himself in that category he dissociates himself from the other possible orientations to ideas. Similarly, the believer recognizes himself as belonging to the category of those who have a special commitment to a particular belief, and at the same time recognizes that there are other people who are also believers but believe in something different. From the latters' point of view he overvalues his belief; but from his point of view, they overvalue theirs. The beliefs of each group of believers are, from the point of view of anyone else who considers the matter, 'over-values'. Finally, to have the 'calculating' orientation towards ideas involves a completely cynical consciousness of the self-interestedness of one's calculation. However as it would not work if one was open about it, this orientation has to be concealed from the world at large.

It is difficult for individuals with a 'calculating' orientation to work in organized groups. It is possible, indeed usual, for individuals with a 'thinking' orientation to join groups whose work consists in 'thinking'. Though they do not *believe* in 'believing', they do, paradoxically, *believe* in thinking, that is to say in a critical and experimental approach to beliefs.

Chapter 6

A CRITIQUE OF 'VALUE'

The believing orientation is to some extent a reaction against the continual flux of the thinking orientation, just as the reverse is true. The speculative activity of thinking does however seem to be a pre-requisite for the formation of group beliefs. Historically, influential systems of belief have arisen *after* a period of diversified thinking.

The believing orientation arose, I suggest, with the second stage of social eidos. In the first stage, each society had its beliefs, and contact between societies was limited, so consciousness of diversity of belief was limited also. Thus the believer only recognized himself as a believer to a very limited extent. But in the second stage the situation was quite different. Not only was there consciousness of diverse cultural traditions, but there was controversy between intellectual schools of thought. In this potentially anomic situation, allegiance to a particular school or group, above all to a particular teacher, offered psychological security. After the initial stage of archaic 'faith', came a stage in which 'faith' and 'reason' alternated, with faith on the whole predominating.

With the rise of the natural sciences and the development of a third stage of social eidos, the believing orientation has undergone further changes. Essentially this was because science appeared to offer a new basis of validity for beliefs. At this stage, more precisely in the mid-eighteenth century, when it was formulated by Kant, the philosophical 'problem of

I   129

value' came into view. The 'problem' was to decide how objectively one could believe in moral truth—in fact, whether such a thing existed or made sense. Kant argued that everyone has a conscience, i.e. a sense that some things are right and some things are wrong; and although they differ in what they think to be right or wrong, they agree in the idea of there being rightness and wrongness. 'Kant was more concerned with the authority and universality of conscience than with the varying and sometimes conflicting forms in which it finds more or less adequate expression; but he was not unaware of the strange and sometimes barbarous customs which have been practised under a mistaken sense of obligation. That was why he insisted on students taking anthropology before turning their attention to ethics.'[1] Kant was, in effect, defending the objectivity of non-specific 'moral value' against the disintegrating effects of rationalist thinking. A long debate followed in intellectual Germany, significant for our analysis of social eidos, because as a result of it the terminology of 'value' ultimately spread to the rest of Europe and America and beyond, both in philosophy and in sociology. We have to inquire whether 'values' are a concept needed in our analysis in addition to those already put forward; and, further whatever we decide about the appropriateness of the concept for our own particular scheme, we are bound to ask why it has become so prominent at the present time.

Kant was anxious to defend 'morality' in the abstract. But so were the rationalist German thinkers who preceded him, especially Wolff (1679–1764), who embodied the confidence in all-embracing 'reason' which the new discoveries of science had inspired. Kant, in effect, claimed that 'moral reason' had an autonomous sphere of its own, separate from the 'reason' of logic and mathematics and from the 'reason' of natural science.

---

[1] A. E. Teale, *Kantian Ethics*, p. 115. In the eighteenth century, 'anthropology' was a general term for human and humanistic studies, including history and psychology.

By distinguishing different kinds of 'rationality' he had, of course, proposed a new meaning for the concept of 'rationality' itself. This idea of a divided rationality was an attempt to make it possible, by a philosophical device, to have 'science' and 'morality' housed in the same world in a general mental climate of reason rather than faith. It was open to attack, however, both by those who thought it showed too little faith in 'faith', in other words was irreligious; and by those who still wanted to make morality a purely cognitive affair. But the debate has been made more complicated by the tendency of some rationalists to be 'on the side of' morality, of others to be on the whole 'against' it.

Comte was a rationalist of the former persuasion. For him the positivist view of science had moral rather than practical or even theoretical value. Theory was superior to practice, and science was superior to industry. 'An intellectual synthesis,' he wrote 'or systematic study of the laws of nature, is needed on far higher grounds than those of satisfying our theoretical faculties, which are, for the most part, very feeble even in men who devote themselves to a life of thought. It is needed, because it solves at once the most difficult problem of the moral synthesis.'[1] In the perspective of Comtean positivism, scientific awareness of the natural, external necessity by which our individual and social existences are ruled is to be the basis of the new social morality: 'the social instincts would never gain the mastery were they not sustained and called into constant exercise by the economy of the external world, an influence which at the same time checks the power of the selfish instincts.'[2] When it first appears on the scene therefore, sociology is the rationale for a science-oriented system of morality.

Comte was, I think, the first writer to place such uncompromising stress on the *social* character of morality. For him, long before Durkheim, the voice of conscience was the voice of 'society'. Perhaps he can even be said to have invented the idea

[1] A. Comte, *Positive Polity*, vol. I, p. 18.　　　　[2] *Ibid.*, p. 17.

of 'society' in the abstract, as a force beyond ourselves. If the consciences of men speak with different voices, this is because they belong to different societies. The evolution of conscience is part and parcel of the evolution of society. Whereas at the 'theological' stage of that evolution, the conscience speaks with the voice of God and religion, at the 'positive' stage, the conscience would speak with the voice of Society and science. Science itself is therefore seen as a 'moral' concept. Its 'value' is not simply rational-technical, nor purely cognitive. It is the advanced expression of social co-operation; and social co-operation is Comte's 'ultimate value'. (Comte does not himself, of course, use the terminology of 'value', but his perspective can be expressed in that terminology because he is essentially a moralist.)

The natural sciences, by upsetting the pre-scientific world-picture and by making possible an increasingly rational-technical way of life, were a threat to traditional morality and therefore to every known kind of morality. They thus threatened, or appeared to threaten, the stability both of the individual personality and of the social fabric. This threat could be met in various ways, for example either by an intensification of 'faith', or, as Kant met it, by postulating a kind of 'morality-in-itself', or 'absolute value', or, as Comte met it, by interpreting science itself in social and moral terms. These were the constructions of men of the 'thinking' orientation, who were convinced that by their 'thinking' they could provide something for 'believers' to believe in, and thus save the integrating idea of belief itself. I suggested, above, that the believing orientation arose with the second stage of social eidos and I am suggesting now that the terminology of 'value' is an expression of the uneasy relationship between what has survived from that stage and the rational-technical tendency of the third stage.

The terminology of value, deriving from Kant and his successors was re-developed in Germany in the second half of the nineteenth century by Dilthey and by the philosophical schools of Marburg and Baden.[1] It was from these philosophers that it passed into the vocabulary of Max Weber. He makes a basic distinction between two types of social behaviour, '*zweckrational*' which means (in its extreme or limiting form) the rational-technical pursuit of one's individual interests, and '*wertrational*', which is defined as 'involving a conscious belief in the absolute value of some ethical, aesthetic, religious, or other form of behaviour, entirely for its own sake and independently of any prospects of external success'[2]. This 'divided rationality' recalls that of Kant and stems from it, though it does not parallel it exactly. The resemblance to Kant lies in the conception that action oriented to an absolute value can be considered rational, but not rational in the same sense as action oriented to one's individual interest. Weber thought that *wertrational* behaviour made up a relatively small part of socially-meaningful behaviour, the bulk of which was what he described as 'traditional' in orientation, shading over into pure automatism. His *wertrational* orientation corresponds broadly, I think, with what I have described above as a 'believing' orientation. What he calls a 'conscious belief' in an 'absolute value' involves what I have called 'believing in belief', in other words the conscious acceptance of an attitude of faith. In his writings on the sociology of religion, Weber worked on the hypothesis that certain 'absolute' or 'ultimate' values were laid down in the ancient civilizations of India and China by *wertrational* individuals and groups, and had entered into the 'traditional' orientation of their societies.

Belief in the value of a particular form of social behaviour is, in the limiting case, conscious, that is to say it is formulated and becomes a social idea, part of the social eidos of the society or group concerned. Weber's use of the terminology of value is, as I see it, broadly interchangeable with the terminology of social eidos and its social structure.

[1] H. A. Hodges, *The Philosophy of Wilhelm Dilthey*, p. 26 *et seq.*
[2] *Theory of Social and Economic Organization*, p. 105.

A CRITIQUE OF 'VALUE'

Durkheim, although he visited Germany in 1885 'to explore the state of philosophical reasearch'[1] did not, in the main body of his work, use the terminology of value. He did, however make constant use of the word 'moral' and he was at heart a moralist in the manner of Comte. The individual, as he saw it, was constrained by the moral forces exerted on him through his social milieu. Without their discipline he would become anomic, purposeless, unstable, prone to depression and suicide. 'As he grew older, Durkheim became more concerned with the breakdown of religion, which he attributed to modern letters, and with the need for more social discipline; suicides seemed to be on the increase and a new social cult was needed to replace weakening religious faith.'[2] He lectured on socialism and was not unsympathetic towards it, but we have no explicit record of his attitude to Marxism as a political movement.[3] He wrote a favourable review of A. Labriola's *Essais sur la conception matérialiste de l'histoire*,[4] and conceptions akin to those of Marx on the relation between ideas and economic and social conditions are to be found in all the writers of the *Année sociologique* and in the British social anthropologists who drew from that source. However if Durkheim had formulated his view of Marxism as a whole it is likely that he would have criticized it on 'moral' grounds, as Comte would have done. And Marxists have been as high-handed with Durkheim as Marx was with Comte. In this context we must take a further look at the attitude of Marx and Marxists to 'morality', and its bearing on the fact that Weber was, both inside and outside his sociology, much less of a 'moralist' than Durkheim.

Hegel in an early essay protested against the 'self-coercion

[1] 'Durkheim: The Man, His Time and His Intellectual Background' by H. Peyre in *ed.* K. Wolff, *Emile Durkheim, 1858–1917*, p. 12.

[2] *Ibid.*, p. 30.

[3] *Ibid.*, 'Durkheim's Politics and Political Theory' by M. Richter, p. 189.

[4] Quoted in the Introduction to *ed.* T. B. Bottomore and M. Rubel, *Karl Marx: Selected Writings*, p. 32.

of Kantian virtue' and described Jesus as 'a spirit raised above morality'.[1] The criticism of morality as deception, bondage, alienation, was a feature of Young Hegelian thought. Marx and Engels accepted this criticism: for them, morality was a bourgeois product, a part of the false consciousness of their time. But they also criticized the critics for conducting their criticism on the plane of philosophy: 'It has not occurred to any one of these philosophers to inquire into the connection of German philosophy with German reality, the relation of their criticism to their own material surroundings.'[2] By arguing about morality, these philosophers diverted attention from German reality and from the need for political action. Though their whole attitude is one of moral indignation, throughout their work Marx and Engels (especially Marx) are, on principle, reticent about moral issues in the abstract. It is only in the earliest writings of Marx, unpublished until long after his death, that one can discern his value-premises, the bases of his social morality.[3] The ultimate aim was to bring to an end man's 'alienation', his subjection to economic and cultural constraint, especially the constraint of money. A very large part of 'morality' was directly concerned with maintaining the property rights and relationships which exercised their crushing constraint on man through a society based on money. Indignation against money morality was the driving force of Marxist thought and action, and made the whole verbal apparatus of morality suspect. But in order to achieve immediate political aims, a laconic morality in which personal interests and desires were subordinated to these aims had to be brought about not by abstract formulation but by organized party discipline. Later, when the party had gained power, the same discipline had to be maintained to carry through the programme of socialist reconstruction and to defend socialism against attack from

---

[1] Quoted by R. Tucker, *Philosophy and Myth in Karl Marx*, p. 40.
[2] K. Marx and F. Engels, *The German Ideology*, p. 6.
[3] R. Tucker, *op. cit.*, p. 123 *et seq.*

within and without. A 'socialist morality', austere and ruthless, thus came into being, almost unadorned by ritual or symbol or by any general airing of ethical principles. In a sense this was the sort of new 'social discipline' that Durkheim thought was needed in France but it was a 'social discipline' without a developed 'social cult'.

The criticism of morality and especially of bourgeois or Philistine morality in Germany was by no means confined to Marx and Marxists. It was expressed, often in tortuous and tormented fashion, in the iconoclastic writings of Schopenhauer and Nietzsche. Though opposed to existing moralities, the idea of morality itself obsessed these thinkers and makes it possible to classify them as moralistic anti-moralists. Max Weber was not moralistic after this pattern. His affinities were more scholarly, rational and liberal. His central concern was with the history and sociology of capitalism. Marx, by emphasizing the economic basis of history, had given a lead to economic historians. In a scholarly sense, Weber was following this lead, amplifying the sparse sociological content of the Marxist historical scheme, and filling in the conceptual gap left by Marxist reticence about 'morality' and 'value'. But Weber himself had something of the same ironic reticence, not so much because he thought moralizing was a poor substitute for political action but because his main motivation was towards greater knowledge and greater objectivity within social eidos. He was emphatic that, though values were part of the subject matter of sociology, the sociologist should himself, in that role, as far as possible be value-free.

The technical, value-free use of the term 'value' *is* possible in sociology. It is a term, however, that since Weber has become associated with a fairly widespread tendency towards what might be called 'moralistic sociologism'. The sociologistic part of this tendency consists in suggesting that the 'social system' is empirically more systematic than it is and that the 'common value system' integrates the social system more definitely than it does. The moralistic part consists in stressing the functional necessity for society of 'morality' as such at all stages of social development.[1]

[1] See Dennis Wrong, 'The Oversocialized Conception of Man in Modern Sociology', *American Sociological Review*, 1961, vol. XXVI, No. 2.

Chapter 7

UN-SOCIAL EIDOS

If one accepts the Freudian view that social morality is partly under the sway of an irrational and primitive super-ego, one may wish to distinguish, within the social self, between that part of it which is so dominated and that part which is guided by the reality principle. The latter part is realistically conscious of its need to belong to a society in order to survive and of its need to accept, in a practical and realistic spirit, the working norms which are socially prescribed. The consciousness of the social self is constructed with the help of social ideas, with elements, that is, from the available social eidos. Each individual works out his individual version of this social self. But it is arguable that at an equally realistic level, each individual could work out—and in fact normally does work out—a consciously un-social self, prepared to resist or evade those social demands which it may consider on realistic grounds to be excessive. Social obligations begin with individuals who are very near to one, and notably in the family, so that the un-social self is bound to be a highly personal and private self, not directly shared. Unshared mental constructions are primitive and shapeless, but indirectly the un-social self *is* shared in the sense that it is built around a set of ideas that have somehow attained a degree of public formulation, for example in art, fiction and humour. The resistance of the conscious self to society is therefore not simply to be identified with laziness, indiscipline, incomplete socialization. A private-self-defending eidos has grown up in interaction with the ideas of social eidos.

Un-social eidos cannot be equated either with the anti-social eidos of criminal groups, nor with 'individualistic' philosophies, at least in the forms they have usually taken. The classic free-enterprise morality, for example, while it seeks to minimize social control by the state, sets up an alternative system of control through money. Super-man moralities of the Nietzschean type call on members of élite groups to revert, as groups, to norms of control through force. The canons of mature un-social eidos are more personal and more elusive. They have taken shape over the past two hundred years largely through the activities of poets, painters and novelists, whose influence has been felt not only through their artistic works and manifestos but through the example of their own private lives.

In his use of the difficult concept of 'alienation', Marx himself had suggested that membership of society subjects man to an alien force, external to himself. It begins with the 'latent slavery in the family' and develops with the social division of labour. 'This crystallization of social activity, this consolidation of what we ourselves produce into an objective power above us, growing out of our control, thwarting our expectations, bringing to naught our calculations, is one of the chief factors in historical development up till now . . . The social power, i.e. the multiplied productive force, which arises through the co-operation of different individuals as it is determined within the division of labour, appears to these individuals, since their co-operation is not voluntary but natural, not as their own united power but as an alien force existing outside them, of the origin and end of which they are ignorant, which they thus cannot control, which on the contrary passes through a peculiar series of phases and stages independent of the will and the action of man, nay even being the prime governor of these.'[1]

Both Marx and Freud were attempting to penetrate beyond conventional and moralistic views of the relationship between

[1] *The German Ideology*, p. 21 *et seq.*

the individual and society. The Marxist concept of alienation emphasizes the externally coercive force of society. The Freudian concept of the super-ego suggests that there is an internally coercive force allied to this externally coercive force. The ultimate ideal of communism is a non-coercive society, but communist society in practice is bound to continue to make coercive demands on its members until there has been a vast and world wide development of material productive forces— otherwise 'the struggle for necessities and all the old filthy business would necessarily be reproduced'.[1] Freud, whose first concern was with the therapy of individuals, for his part found himself 'obliged to do battle with the super-ego', and warned that 'exactly the same objections can be made against the ethical standards of the cultural super-ego'.[2] Beyond their criticism of the contemporary social moralities of money and sex respectively there was a more fundamental criticism of society itself, and the groundwork of a potential theory and programme for the socially controlled relaxation and liberalization of the social bond.

[1] *Ibid.*, p. 24.   [2] *Civilization and its Discontents*, p. 139.

Chapter 8

THE RATIONALITY OF SURVIVAL

In looking ahead to this possibility, one cannot forget that the human world as a whole is in the grip of technical problems of survival and that the dominant outlook is the technical outlook. All other facts look insignificant beside the growth of human populations and the task of feeding them and supplying their basic needs. This problem will be the over-riding one as far ahead as we can see. As a result, economic and technical development remains, for the world as a whole, a first priority. Moreover, it is evident that scientists, who have already contributed so much to this development have poten-tially a far greater contribution still to make. So far as general eidos and its social structure are concerned, we can only imagine that it will become more and more technical-rational as time goes on. If there is to be any shift within social eidos and its social structure, this can only be in the context of a general orientation towards the eidos of the applied sciences.

Technical rationality is the appropriate rationality for the control of physical nature. It depends on social co-operation as on any other tool. As constituent parts of a system of co-operation, economic, political or social—men are, in a familiar phrase, 'cogs in a machine'. In consenting to be cogs, they are rational towards their great tool, society. But this rationality may be masking their irrationality towards their 'selves', biologic-ally and psychologically. Rational understanding of the human mind and body, their interaction with each other and with the environment and its potentialities, is one-sided because it has been developed so largely in a context of concern with fitness for socially 'useful' activities. In those favoured societies of tomorrow which have a sufficient surplus of wealth and leisure, there could be more time than at present for activities of mind and body which, though 'useless', are satisfying in themselves, in which, for example, there is a high athletic or aesthetic component. A man can 'use' his mind and body as a tool, it is true, but he can also feel and imagine through them, which he cannot do through other tools. Body and mind, once they have been liberated, at least partially, from the tyranny of the environment have still to be liberated from the subtler tyrannies which society, morality and science itself exercise over them for their own 'good'.

Almost everything has still to be learnt about what is possible in this direction. The possibilities may well vary from one individual to another, even at a biological level. We cannot plan for a society in which everyone would be an artist, or an athlete, or a pure scientist. The designers of utopias are themselves in all probability conditioned not only by their cultural background but by their physique.[1] Even more difficult to overcome will be the preconceptions inherent in words like society, morality, value, beauty, art, science and rationality itself. Freud has helped us to see how at the very moment when we think ourselves most rational we are motivated by irrational impulses. The full bearing of this on many of our socially sanctioned and approved activities will not be clear without far-reaching extension of psychological knowledge and understanding.

At each stage of social eidos a dominant orientation of thought has tended to limit and shackle the freedom of social perceptions. This limitation has been so pervasive that so long as it has

[1] Compare W. H. Sheldon, *The Varieties of Human Physique* and (with S. S. Stevens) *The Varieties of Temperament*; H. J. Eysenck, *Structure of Human Personality*; R. W. Parnell, *Behaviour and Physique*.

lasted, societies have been so to speak locked into institutional moulds and fixities. The shaking of the structure and the changing of the social eidos have proceeded in parallel. The rate and direction of structural change has at least partly depended on the invention, diffusion and acceptance of new long-term perspectives and ideal goals. A change in type of teleological scheme has in fact been the crucial development at each new stage of social eidos.

Chapter 9

OTHER RATIONALITIES?

In attempting to look beyond the present stage, one has not so much a 'vision' of the future' as fragments of utopias that do not seem to fit together. In an earlier chapter, I speculated that philosophers and psychologists might presently suggest a meaning for 'rationality' which would extend beyond the instrumental meaning which it has acquired in an age dominated by the applied use of science. I cannot however imagine a new kind of rationality which would *not* include and comprehend this rationality which we have built up with so much difficulty, the rationality, one might say, of human survival. Pareto defined the 'practical purpose of human beings' as 'the welfare and prosperity of themselves and their societies.' What other rationale could there be for the exercise of rationality? If there are other rationalities, a precondition for them is the rationality of survival.

This rationality, I take it, is the rationality identified by Gaston Bachelard as having 'utility for life' as opposed to 'utility for the mind'. He believes that scientists of genius, by 'psycho-analysing' their own cognitive processes, can achieve, by a 'psychological mutation', a way of scientific thinking in terms of 'utility for the mind', even if this involves thinking not 'with' but 'against' the human brain.[1] It is necessary, he says, for the advanced scientific mind to conquer completely its anthropomorphic tendency, to banish all human values from

[1] G. Bachelard, *La Formation de l'Esprit Scientifique*, p. 251.

144

its universe. Eventually everyone must be educated to think in this way, and the life-long 'school' in which they do so will be the *raison d'être* of society rather than the other way round as at present.

This vision of a pure scientific rationality cultivated for its own sake at the expense of every other type of perception has at least the merit of an extreme solution. It is at the opposite extreme from that proposed by Norman O. Brown and Herbert Marcuse, whose vision is of a revolutionary reconciliation between cerebral man and his sensual body.[1] What these psychological utopias have in common is release from the constraint of technological rationality—the eidos of our time—without recourse to mystical or 'moral' solutions which would be a regression to earlier stages of eidos.

If one were to take either of these visions seriously in terms of the deliberate attempt to construct a social structure of social eidos through which the vision could be realized, there are obvious difficulties, not only in the transition but in the completed structure. Unless one were to breed a population of pure minds or pure bodies, the variability of individuals would mean that the 'ultimate value' of the society was truly meaningful only for a minority, and that the rest of the society would be carrying on as before, on a 'practical' basis, concerned with welfare and prosperity, with the additional task of making possible the special activities of the dedicated minorities.

[1] See above, p. 92.

Chapter 10

THE AESTHETIC UTOPIA

The ideal goal for society as a whole, if we imagine it as based firmly on the foundation of material welfare for all of its members and as providing a *moyen de vivre* for its exceptional members and meta-social minorities, still seems to lack the final stamp of value for its own sake in a form that all can grasp. If this value is to be derived from the non-coercive elements of the anthropomorphic human mind, it will be aesthetic rather than moral. In his early philosophical manuscripts, writes Tucker 'Marx's conception of ultimate communism is fundamentally *aesthetic* in character. His utopia is an aesthetic ideal of the future man-nature relationship, which he sees in terms of artistic creation and the appreciation of the beauty of the man-made environment by its creator. The acquisitive and therefore alienated man of history is to be succeeded by the post-historical aesthetic man who will be "rich" in a new way. Marx describes him as "the *rich* man profoundly endowed with all the senses", adding: "The *rich* human being is simultaneously the human being *in need* of a totality of human life-activities". In Marx's view, the relationship of this new man to nature— that is, to his own anthropological nature—will be that of an artist. Man will realize his natural tendency to arrange things "according to the laws of beuty! Economic activity will turn into artistic activity . . . and the planet itself will become the new man's work of art. The alienated world will give way to the aesthetic world'.[1]

[1] R. Tucker, *Philosophy and Myth in Karl Marx*, p. 157.

THE AESTHETIC UTOPIA

In the mature writings on which political Marxism is based, Marx is concerned with the economics and politics of the revolutionary transition and says very little about the ultimate utopia. This silence is in keeping with his mood of sticking close to the harsh contemporary realities which had been obscured by nineteenth century false consciousness. Another economist and realist, Pareto, who stressed the non-rational origin of all values, was himself, as Parsons has well written, 'a lover of civilization', by which 'he meant the flowering of literature, the arts, science and the like such as occurred in classical Athens or in Renaissance Italy. Such a flowering, he held, was not associated with any static state of society, but with the stage in the process of the disintegration of the persistence of aggregates in favour of the combinations residues. The "lions"[1] are generally of such strong faith as to be fanatics. They create an atmosphere of rigid orthodoxy, intolerance, binding ritual, austerity of discipline and sometimes other-worldliness which stifles civilization. That requires an atmosphere of relative freedom, tolerance, mobility. Thus Pareto repeatedly states that a flowering of civilization is associated with an increase in the combinations residues.[2] But when the process goes so far as to break down the "barbarous" rigidity of fanaticism it soon proceeds to the point of endangering the stability of the society in which civilization flourishes. Perhaps, though Pareto does not say so, too much instinct of combinations is fatal to the arts in itself. But however that may be, a new wave of fanaticism may wipe out the creations of the previous cycle which has to start over again to a large extent. Thus according to Pareto's view of civilization, its flowering has taken place only under certain specific conditions which have been in the nature of the case of short duration and have been closely linked with occurrences that are repugnant to most lovers of the fruits of civilization. The grimness and

[1] The 'lions', in Pareto's version of the fable, are the 'new men' rising from lower strata in society to replace the corrupt 'foxes' of the upper strata.   [2] V. Pareto, *The Mind and Society*, § 2345, 2529 ff.

147

fanaticism of the "lions" are generally a prelude, however unpleasant it may be, and the regime of fraud and corruption the usual end product of the total process'.[1]

It seemed to Pareto that although science and technology might progress, the cyclical tendencies in society prevented it from attaining, as a final state, the kind of 'civilization' that he valued. Ages of faith were bound to alternate with ages of reason. Reason and faith were elements in the social process which must both be reckoned with as permanent factors. The most he would allow was the possibility of an optimum proportion or relationship between the two, and the even remoter possibility of a sociology that could determine and control this proportion. Given this very remote possibility, he would according to his own values have looked forward to a society where the arts were cultivated as well as the sciences. Classical Athens and Renaissance Italy, which he so much admired, were remarkable among other things, for an aesthetic development in which the value of the human body, male or female, was accepted without puritanism.[2] To Pareto, 'civilization' meant not the renunciation of the value of the body but a liberal culture based upon it—a civilization *without* its discontents.

One may wonder, indeed, whether the arts can ever again develop to the pitch of intensity which they achieved in the past, before the dis-anthropomorphizing effect of scientific rationality made itself fully felt. 'At a single blow' writes Bachelard 'it is our whole universe which is robbed of its colour, it is our whole sustenance which loses its savour, it is our whole natural psychic élan which is broken, reversed, laid under suspicion and demoralized. We had so great a need to put our entire selves inside our vision of the world. But it is precisely that need which we have to conquer.'[3] The mathematical physicist needs to shed every anthropomorphic tendency in his

[1] T. Parsons, *The Structure of Social Action*, p. 292.
[2] In *Le Mythe Vertuiste*, Pareto criticizes the hypocrisy of bourgeois crusades against sexual immorality.   [3] *Op. cit.*, p. 24.

thought; but he, perhaps, can afford to be philosophical about it. In other spheres of thought and action, the anthropomorphic concepts are not replaced by mathematical formulae, but are left, devalued and threadbare, an obsolete language for which there is no substitute. Can we ever reinvent a 'vision of the world' which will satisfy us aesthetically, or shall we have to hoard, as long as we can, the aesthetic capital we inherit from classical Athens, Renaissance Italy and other past 'flowerings'? Are the arts to become a 'dead language', whose meaning can only be relearnt by a reconstruction of the kind of life that was lived in the pre-scientific stages of civilization?

I think the decision-makers of future societies will be involved in deliberate social decisions about the relative dominance to be allowed (in education, for example) to the part of the human mind which has moved furthest from its anthropomorphic base and the part which acknowledges the force of the promptings of the body. The two appear to be irreconcilable, and if we grant that we cannot dispense with either, then some sort of balance between them will be sought if compromise is possible. I would like to be able to suggest a basis on which a conscious compromise could be made. But I feel that we still know too little about the fundamental biology and psychology of human behaviour to provide such a basis. I can only pay homage to the clarification which a few thinkers, most of all Pareto and Freud, have seemed to me to bring to the question.

Freud also had his personal values and preconceptions. He had a strong belief in the beneficent value of science in the service of human welfare, and he set art side by side with science as the product of human striving 'towards the two convergent aims of profit and pleasure'. Culture, whose two purposes are 'protecting humanity against nature' and 'regulating the relations of human beings among themselves', is, in spite of the rational achievements on which it prides itself, far from being a purely rational construction. The fact that 'the lack of beauty is a thing we cannot tolerate in civilization' shows that

149

'culture is not simply utilitarian'. The civilization of a country is judged partly by the extent to which it is 'exploiting the earth for man's benefit' and 'protecting him against nature'. But 'we count it also as proof of a high level of civilization when we see that the industry of the inhabitants is applied as well to things which are not in the least useful and, on the contrary, seem to be useless, e.g. when the parks and gardens in a town, which are necessary as playgrounds and air-reservoirs, also bear flowering plants, or when the windows of dwellings are adorned with flowers. We soon become aware that the useless thing which we require of civilization is beauty'.[1]

There is, he says again, 'no very evident use in beauty; the necessity of it for cultural purposes is not apparent *and yet civilization could not do without it*. The science of aesthetics investigates the conditions in which things are regarded as beautiful; it can give no explanation of the nature or origin of beauty; as usual, its lack of results is concealed under a flood of resounding and meaningless words. Unfortunately, psycho-analysis, too, has less to say about beauty than about most things. Its derivation from the realms of sexual sensation is all that seems certain'.[2] The value of sexual sensation itself was, of course, what it was Freud's life work to emphasize. 'It is impossible to ignore' he wrote 'the extent to which civilization is built up on renunciation of instinctual gratifications, the degree to which the existence of civilization presupposes the non-gratification (suppression, repression or something else?) of powerful instinctual urgencies. This "cultural privation" dominates the whole field of social relations between human beings; we know already that it is the cause of the antagonism against which all civilization has to fight.'[3] The sense of privation caused by the suppression of instincts expresses itself in 'the cry for freedom . . . directed either against particular forms or demands of culture or else against culture itself. It does not seem as if man could be

[1] S. Freud, *Civilization and its Discontents*, p. 54.
[2] *Ibid.*, p. 38, my italics. [3] *Ibid.*, p. 63.

brought by any sort of influence to change his nature into that of the ants; he will always, one imagines, defend his claim to individual freedom against the will of the multitude. A great part of the struggles of mankind centres round the single task of finding some expedient (i.e. satisfying) solution between these individual claims and those of the civilized community; it is one of the problems of man's fate whether this solution can be arrived at in some particular form of culture or whether the conflict will prove irreconcilable'.[1]

In these speculative and musing pages, Freud allows for the *possibility*—he puts it no higher—that society might be so reorganized as to reduce 'cultural privation' while maintaining a scientific control over the environment. As to the part which might be played in this by the arts and by 'the aesthetic attitude' he does not seem certain. 'Those who are sensitive to the influence of art do not know how to rate it high enough as a source of happiness and consolation in life. Yet art affects us but as a mild narcotic and can provide no more than a temporary refuge for us from the hardships of life; its influence is not strong enough to make us forget real misery.'[2] 'The substitute gratifications, such as art offers, are illusions in contrast to reality, *but none the less satisfying to the mind on that account*, thanks to the place which phantasy has reserved for herself in mental life.'[3] Art as an illusion, a narcotic, a substitute gratification, can hardly recommend itself to a psycho-analyst bent on bringing his patient to terms with reality. Art, like the other 'higher mental operations', scientific and ideological, is made possible by the 'sublimation of instinct'. Surely 'cultural privation' would not be reduced by aesthetic sublimation but only by a radical de-repression of the instinct itself, is what Freud seems to be saying. Yet he also warns, cryptically, that 'it would be better to reflect a little longer' on the proposition that 'sublimation is a fate which has been forced upon instincts by culture alone'.

[1] *Ibid.*, p. 61.   [2] *Ibid.*, p. 35.   [3] *Ibid.*, p. 25, my italics.

There is a genuine puzzle in Freud's thought here, a puzzle which must remain unsolved until we have a more adequate knowledge of what we mean by 'sublimation' and 'substitute gratification', and even by such fundamental concepts as 'phantasy' and 'instinct'. There is some sense, Freud feels, in which art is not an 'illusion' in the same way as religion, perhaps because art does not pretend to be anything else but illusion. Religion, like science, claims to be in touch with reality. In the case of religion, Freud did not admit the truth of this claim, though he accepted it in the case of science. From another point of view, however, which he well recognized, art is in touch with a sphere of mental reality in which illusions *are* true.

Is it the case, as Freud says, that 'civilization could not do without' this sphere, or can we psycho-analyse ourselves out of dependence on any means of contact with it? Can we become pure minds, and outgrow our anthropomorphic body-minds? If we do so, we are, as Bachelard clearly sees, rejecting our bodies also, like the Hindu sages in the final stages of their enlightenment. If we choose not to reject our bodies, then we choose also to live with our anthropomorphic minds, reserving the exploits of the pure mind for the adepts of advanced cognition. The value of the body, not as a tool only but as a mode of feeling, and the value of the anthropomorphic mind and its perceptions, artistic, pre-scientific and proto-scientific, may one day become as much a deliberate part of civilization as the value of survival and the value of pure cognition.

In conclusion, it may be in order to ask what purpose if any has been served by Part III of this book and by the mode of discussion it has adopted. What has been added by it to the reader's awareness and in what possible way might it affect his activities?

Potentially, critical discussion of the underlying assumptions of social eidos, of sociology and of social thinking in general, may liberate and motivate human energies for work in new directions. These directions are barred at present by habit and inertia, by utilitarian priorities, by the dilution of religious faith, by sociologism, and so on. For sociology and social psychology, the foregoing discussions imply a programme for studying the social structure of social eidos, and the elements of social eidos, the social values of societies and groups and the modes of their diffusion. The identification and clarification of social assumptions and of the social structure within which they are carried and with which they are enmeshed, through sociological inquiry, is likely in my view to have a liberating effect in every field of human activity. Only by recognizing the assumptions by which our activities are ultimately governed can we begin consciously to modify them.

INDEX

155

INDEX

INDEX

Kant, I., 95, 109, 129, 130, 132, 133, 135
Kepler, J., 48
Keynes, J. M., 48

Labriola, A., 134
Lenin, V. I., 65
Le Play, F., 62 n.
Lévy-Bruhl, L., 20, 21, 22, 23, 25, 28, 31, 98 n.
Linton, R., 100 n.
Littré, E., 61 n.
Locke, J., 47
Lotze, R. H., 95
Lucian, 79
Lumholtz, C., 25

Magic, 22, 23, 43, 44, 48, 49, 80
Malinowski, B., 20, 22
Mannheim, K., 70, 106, 116, 117, 118, 121
Marcuse, H., 16, 92, 145
Marx, K., 14, 16, 31, 58, 60–68, 70–72, 81, 94, 110, 113–17, 134, 135, 136, 139, 140, 146, 147
Mass-communication, 104, 122
Mathematics, 43, 49, 51 n., 130, 148
Mead, G., 100 n.
Mencius, 40
Merton, R. K., 48
Mesopotamia, 31, 32, 41
Metaphysic, 50, 51 n., 62, 63, 65 n., 69
Money, 56, 135, 139, 140
Morality, 44, 52 n., 55, 58, 90, 93, 101, 109, 130, 131, 132, 134, 135, 136, 137, 140, 142, 145
Myrdal, G., 85 n.
Mysticism, 20, 21, 22, 23, 24, 26, 42, 43, 48, 55, 145
Myth, 22, 31, 35, 49, 73, 74

Nadel, S. F., 100 n.
Napoleon, 65 n.
Needham, J., 16, 41 n., 48

Neo-Kantians, 95
Newton, I., 48
Nietszche, F., 42, 95, 136, 139
Norms, 81, 97, 98, 138, 139
Nuer, 25, 27

Orphism, 43

Pareto, V., 16, 20, 49, 50 n., 58, 73, 74–90, 93, 98, 102, 110, 116, 125, 144, 147, 148, 149
Parnell, R. W., 142 n.
Parsons, T., 16, 59, 73, 75, 94–106, 109, 116, 118, 127, 147
Peirce, C. S., 98 n.
Peyre, H., 134
Philosophy, 36, 38, 40, 41, 42, 43, 45, 51 n., 94, 130, 135
Plato, 43
Poetry, 29, 30, 49, 139
Politics, 55, 56, 57, 65, 80, 105, 115, 123, 147; scientific, 58, 71, 106
Popper, K., 51 n., 71 n.
Positivism, 50, 51, 58, 62, 63, 131
Progress, idea of, 50, 55, 57, 74
Protestant Ethic, 99
Psycho-analysis, 150, 151, 152
Psychology, 16, 57, 58, 78, 102, 113, 119, 141, 142; social, 153; psychological utopia, 145, 149
Puritanism, 48, 148
Pythagoras, 43

Radcliffe-Brown, A., 21, 96 n.
Radin, P., 20, 22, 23
Rationality, 69, 74, 89, 93, 131, 142, 144, 145; scientific, 145; of survival, 15, 110, 141, 144; technical, 14, 46, 47, 55, 57, 72, 109, 132, 133, 141
Reformation, Protestant, 46, 51 n.
Religion, 22, 23, 25, 26, 27, 28, 29, 30, 33, 36, 43, 45, 47, 48, 50, 55, 69, 73, 75, 80, 87, 90, 93, 104, 109, 115, 120 n., 123, 132, 133, 134, 152

INDEX

Residues, 76–79, 81–84, 87, 89, 147; classification of, 82
Revolution, Chinese, 72; French, 60, 72; Russian, 72
Richter, M., 134
Riesman, D., 100 n.
Ritschl, A., 95
Role expectations, 97, 100, 102, 103
Rome, 45

Saint-Pierre, Abbe de, 47
Saint-Simon, H. de, 50, 60
Scheler, M., 95
Schopenhauer, A., 136
Science, 41 n., 42, 43, 44, 45–52, 55, 56, 58, 72, 78, 80, 84, 110, 129, 130, 131, 132, 141, 142, 144, 148, 149, 152; social, 51, 105, 106, 118
Sentiment, 77, 79, 84, 115
Sex, 80, 83, 89, 90, 91, 140, 150
Shamanism, 23, 24, 37, 41 n., 43, 44
Sheldon, W. H., 142 n.
Simmel, G., 95, 98 n.
Social action, 96, 99
Social structure, 27, 110, 111, 112, 115, 116, 118, 143
Social system, 96, 97, 103, 136
Socialism, 63, 75, 80, 90, 134, 135
Sociology, 51 n., 58, 71, 81, 93, 117, 130, 131, 136, 148, 152, 153; of knowledge, 70
Sorel, G., 74
Spinoza, 51 n.
Stevens, S. S., 142 n.
Stirner, M., 69, 70
Strauss, D. F., 69
Stuart Hughes, H., 73 n.
Super-ego, 89, 92, 100, 101, 102, 138, 140; cultural, 35, 126, 140

Taoism, 34, 40, 41

Teachers, great, 34, 35, 36, 37, 38, 44, 45, 46, 51 n., 93, 129
Teale, A. E., 130 n.
Thales, 42, 43
Theology, 24, 40, 43, 46, 50, 51, 52, 69, 73, 99, 132
Theory, logico-experimental, 77; and practice, 64, 131
Totemism, 21, 24, 26, 69
Tucker, R., 135 n., 146
Turgot, A. R. J., 50
Tylor, E., 43

Upanishads, 34, 37, 38
Universities, 46, 114, 117, 118 n., 121
Utopia, 63, 142, 144, 145, 147; *see also* aesthetic utopia

Valat, F., 61, 64
Values, 81, 94–104, 109, 111, 129, 132, 133, 134, 136, 142, 146, 148, 149, 152; ultimate, 44, 97, 99, 100, 110, 145
Vico, G., 29, 30, 31
Voltaire, F. M. A. de, 47, 51 n.
Vote, 56

Waley, A., 40
Weber, M., 16, 48, 73, 94, 95, 96, 98, 100, 102, 114, 127, 133, 134, 136
Wirth, L., 13 n.
Wolff, C., 130
Wolff, K., 134
Wrong, D., 137
Wundt, W., 98 n.

Yoga, 38, 39, 41

Zoroastrianism, 34